SOBER IS BETTER

MY NOTE TO SELF

BRYAN WEMPEN

INHERITANCE
PRESS

INHERITANCE
P R E S S

Published by Inheritance Press LLC
Lake Mary, Florida 32746
www.inheritancepress.com

Cover design — Tom Morse-Brown
Bio photo — David K. Pugh
Cover painting — "Thoughts" by Bryan Wempen (2017)
Critique and copy editor — Keidi Keating
Last minute editor — Meghan Flanigan

Library of Congress Control Number: 2019938717

ISBN: 978-0-9823859-9-9

Printed in the United States of America

To Michella
Your quiet courage, strength, and support
make me better.

Contents

Acknowledgements

MY FAMILY IS MENTIONED A LOT in the book; I know they did their best based on their experience and life. I'm grateful for them in my life.

To everyone who inspired and supported me as I wrote this book, thank you. What a range of people, places, and things are involved in translating thoughts to story, especially my ridiculously talented team (Monique, Tom, Keidi, Meghan, Tobie, Michella). A special hug for Michael, Alicia, Laurie, Jay, and Chris.

Grateful for a thousand hours of music into my ears, helping me focus and distract myself while I wrote: Linkin Park, Colin Hay, Macklemore, Lady Gaga/Brad Cooper, Demi Lovato, X Ambassadors, Nothing But Thieves, Banners, Shylah Ray Sunshine, Ruth B., Tom Walker, Satsang, Shakira, Jamison Ross, Rag'n'Bone, Dua Lipa, and Fitz and The Tantrums.

Inspired by the writings of authors when I am writing. It feels good to connect with the flow of other ideas and stories. Anna David, Brené Brown, Ryan Hampton, Lisa Johnson, Bill Wilson, Kevin Hart, Rick Hanson, Ernest Kurtz, Father Gregory Boyle, Bobbi Jo Reed, Sam Quinones, Steven Pressfield, Brian Cuban, Trevor Noah, Lane Moore, Sheryl Sandberg/Adam Grant, Chris Difford, Charles Duhigg, Kate Bowler, Andrew Sean Greer, Amy Dresner, Sarah Hepola, Bill Clegg, and Kelley Kitley.

Preface

As the words spill onto a page, I often get emotional while pounding out my thoughts, feelings, and experiences on the keyboard about getting sober and finding what matters in life. I get emotional because I'm blessed to have the opportunity share my experience, strength, and hope with anyone that will listen or read about it.

Without recovery my life changes significantly; at minimum it's an empty life, most likely I'm not alive today. I was spiraling out of control until the day I surrendered my will about my ability to drink normally. My admitting I was out of control, that I needed help to survive this life thing was the single hardest moment. I'm just willing enough to initiate a change in my drinking and thinking because I'm in emotional pain. My life started again that day. It was a solution that wasn't quick, easy, or dichotomous in nature.

This book is comprised of two parts:

Part One—Me sharing of my early years' story before and into becoming dependent on alcohol. It's basically my first 18 years on this earth. This part is written in more of a narrative and story form. The early years part of the book is before addiction, before every day was a battle NOT to use something to change my feelings. It takes you the reader into my before and during, utterly sinking into alcohol addiction in every sense.

Part Two—Is a collection of shorter stories about lessons learned in recovery from alcohol and drugs. These are my experiences with living sober and not—these stories are my therapy sessions. I suppose one could call it "sharapy." I'm hoping to have lots of people join me in my session work by reader and discuss what's going on with their life. Some experiences, fears, and emotions were much harder to share and write about than others. These were the ones I'll be unsure about even as the book comes off the press. I need to write about these things; I've been holding on to some of them for a long time.

How about empathizing and cheering as loudly as we can for those who are trying and moving successfully through addiction, tragedy, and trauma. We have experienced loss, healing, and recovery. Keep going, start over when necessary, never stop until you get to that light, a place we find calm and peace in many forms of recovery.

I understand you could be doing several other things rather than reading my book; your time is significant and valuable. I'm honored and grateful you're with me on my journey.

Kindly,
Bryan Wempen

Foreword

"Starting over isn't a failure; it's a smarter beginning."

I'VE ALWAYS LOVED THESE WORDS FROM Bryan Wempen's first book, Note to Self. We still have a choice, we always have it in us to improve our lives, and how we approach the world, we can always do better for ourselves and others. Bryan's mission in life is to strive to achieve this daily, and generously to share his words so as to help others along the way.

It has been my honour, privilege, and pleasure to know Bryan for the best part of a decade. His words, his thoughts, his values inspire me constantly. However, I have only met him in real life the once (in a publisher's office near the banks of the Thames in London, on a swelteringly hot day some years back). My friendship with Bryan came about thanks to Twitter. The written word, whether shared in 140 (then 280) character tweets or book form can create powerful connections. Your outlook on life — your life itself — can be informed, changed, improved by these words. Our friendship continues to this day, enabled by social media, email and the written word. I cherish this friendship. I gain so much from it.

Gentle reader, I envy you having the opportunity to read Sober is Better, a Note to Self still ahead of you. Bryan writes compellingly, movingly and with great humour of his struggles with addiction (first with drugs, then with alcohol — an "equal opportunity killer that indiscriminately comforts us right up to the point it doesn't any longer," as Bryan puts it), and of how his complex early life lead him there. He hit rock bottom on Sunday 9 May 2010. He realised that he could go no further down this path. It was time to seek help. To opt for a new beginning, a smarter beginning. "My life started again that day," he writes. "We all deserve as many chances as it takes to live the best life we can possibly live."

Bryan is clear-eyed about how life leads him here, and about where he would like to go from here. He takes full responsibility for his life as an addict. He takes full responsibility for his journey of recovery. He relishes the challenges that life has gifted him: to remain sober; to overcome self-doubt, self-hatred, self-destruction; to love and to share. Moreover, to approach this whole business of life itself with joy, with humour. Bryan writes: "My simple goals each day stay sober, laugh a lot, and love as much as possible."

The words that Bryan chooses to share in this book are of great potential value to us all, whether addiction has touched our lives, or otherwise. Each of us has a choice, always. We can choose to approach each day as a possible "smarter beginning" to the rest of our lives. Here is another phrase from Bryan's first book that has stuck with me ever since I first read it: "Today I'm doing the next right thing." Is there any better goal for every one of us than always to try to do the next right thing?

The voice you hear speak to you through these pages is uniquely Bryan's. Full of wit, warmth, and wisdom. The voice of a friend. I hope that reading his words will inspire you to look a little differently at your own life, your challenges. To see each moment as a smarter beginning.

Michael Carty
February 2019

Sober Is Better: Part One

HI, MY NAME IS BRYAN, I'm in long-term recovery, sober from drugs and alcohol. I stopped using drugs 22 years ago, then drinking alcohol 10 years ago. I share my early story to provide a little more about me. About me, being adopted, growing up on a farm, and finally heading to university. I jump then to several short stories and thoughts on life before and after recovery. My hope is my perspective with failures and successes getting sober then being sober, resonates with someone. It's possible for anyone to find healing in some form, recovery from a darkness that has engulfed our lives. Whether it's someone in your family, friend or you; I hope my story helps to make sense of what I know from experience feels impossible at times.

The Mayo Clinic describes AUD as the following: "Alcohol use disorder (which includes a level that's sometimes called alcoholism) is a pattern of alcohol use that involves problems controlling your drinking, being preoccupied with alcohol, continuing to use alcohol even when it causes problems, having to drink more to get the same effect, or having withdrawal symptoms when you rapidly decrease or stop drinking."

I'm excited and honored for you to be reading my book. The details are from my memory of the events in my life, I'm sure some are more accurate than others. All my writing is in the spirit of my best recollection the events and my attempt to convey something that might resonate with where you are at in your life.

Foremost, I'm requesting as my family and friends, who well might be the only ones who read the book, please remember that addiction and trauma impact us all. These two things touch the lives of you and everyone you know if you don't believe me just start asking people about it.

In the book I share more about addiction than trauma as it affected me; both things impact lives of our family, friends, employees, co-workers, teachers, students, doctors, coaches, drivers, clergy, politicians, and every other group. We are losing our fellows hour by hour at record levels in 2019 drugs and alcohol related death. It was the first year the data supported that drug overdoses are more lethal than auto accidents. Many who research addiction and recovery have known for a long time that drug and alcohol-related deaths were much higher than dying in a car crash; finally, this public health crisis is center stage for all to help.

The only positive I'm able to glean from the crisis is hearing the story of someone who'd found recovery. Finding your light back from the hopelessness is hard, and some refer to this as a living miracle.

"More often the stopping point is the starting point."

— TOM HERZOG, ENDING STIGMA ADVOCATE

Chapter 1

Stories We Tell

I'M SITTING IN MY BEDROOM AT age 7 when it occurs to me that I must be from northern Italy and a real Italian. I had read that this region had many blonde and blue-eyed Italians; real or not, it only made sense this was my unknown heritage. It was one of the many stories I convinced myself and others of for many years because I'm adopted. I knew virtually nothing about myself for 25 more years.

This persona I created to ease some of the internal emotional torment that comes from a feeling of detachment and unworthiness lasted for more than half my life. Creating several personas ended up being one of my best emotional survival skills. This skill of sharing fictional realities continued well into recovery as an adult.

Many years later I do learn more about biological history from my birth mother, who I meet first by phone, then in real life. What a shock when I found out my self-created stories of being Italian was all wrong. I'm a lot Scottish, French, Irish, and English. This was only half my background, it was 2019 almost 15 years later I'd learn the rest. This new other half was not the least bit dull, a few twists and turns.

My objective upon meeting my birth mother for the first time was to ask specific questions I'd always planned on asking. This of course was if the conversation ever did happen, until it did, I'd never planned on it. When it did go down, I found my questions normal in my mind because I'm relatively quirky and funny, they were enough to break the ice from this quite emotional conversation. Questions as follows in order of priority for me at this time in my life:

a)   Is there male pattern baldness in the family?

b)   Am I Jewish? I'd always wanted to be Jewish. I'm not on this side of the family.

c)   Do any major health issues in the family exist I need to know about. Nothing major, minus the propensity for substance use disorder which we all learned more about years later.

In my 33 years I had prayed for the ability to do one thing as it related to my biological mother, it was to tell her, Thank you. I'm empathetic to a decision of that magnitude, it was likely complicated and hard to make, and my life turned out alright based on your decision back then. This was a conversation I had about eight years before I got sober. My life was kind of a complete wreck, best way to put it. It was still a life that I was navigating but trust me I know how much worse it could have always been. I'm grateful that day anyway for what I had.

I was adopted within 2 days of being born; this is a significant part of my story. My knowledge was minimal about who, what, and where my history consisted. Just as I experienced later in my addiction, I had emotional gaps I was driven to fill one way or another in my life. I'd then learn adoption is a more likely substantial part of my addiction, recovery, and story than I'd given it credit. I revisit this several times throughout the book, it's how it all started.

My simple goals each day: stay sober, laugh a lot, and love as much as possible. It is laughing at myself and at life because so much in life is ridiculous, beautiful, and funny. Recently, even after years in recovery, I forgot that laughing was one of my goals. Even now after years in long-term recovery, it requires practice to achieve my little but essential daily goals. Ok, let's all laugh it up right now, see if it makes you feel better. Laughing also burns calories, that's always a bonus!

Laughing and loving are tied as my second most essential priorities after staying sober. While writing this book, it didn't take long for my addict brain to start telling me how life isn't that great. This wasn't true, but my mind lies to me occasionally. In recovery, I've learned emotional tools and have a network of people to remind me these thoughts are my disease of addiction, lying to me again. My life is quite fantastic today, and a considerable part of my life is growing my relationships with those I care. I probably took a break while writing this book, many times, to spend some time with those important to me.

12-Steps

I got sober using a combination of things, primarily it was the 12-steps of Alcoholics Anonymous. AA was my thing before therapy, before breathwork, meditation, and spiritual practices. I've attended 800 meetings across about 20 different states in 10 years, it wouldn't have hurt for me to hit a few more. Some of these meetings are close to what you might of saw in the movies, others not that similar. They all have three things in common-coffee, alcoholics, and people trying to get better. State by state, city by city, and meeting by meeting it's all mostly similar and a little different on how they go about things.

The first meeting I attended was years before I got sober, 13 years before to be accurate, then 6 years later a few times. I ultimately walked into a meeting in Tulsa, Oklahoma, a speaker meeting in a church, AA coffee, people greeting at the door-ask me if it was my first time. This time I said yes, it was my first time I would do anything to get clean. I've got a lifetime of gratitude for AA. It helped save my life, it's helped save other lives, and it's also not for everyone. That's alright, find your recovery whatever it takes! We don't want to lose you.

The speaker was Kathy, her story was amazing, I cried the entire meeting because I sound like her, her story was my story. It felt like I finally fit into a group. This was 10 years ago, I still go to A.A. along with many things to help me maintain and grow my recovery program. I am a fan of A.A. but always aware it's not the only way to save your life from drugs, alcohol, gambling, porn, food, work, and sex. MAT, hard reduction, and various therapy programs. Thank you to all my sponsors whether they knew it or not, Randy, X, Seth, Jeannie, Heather, Bill, and Matt.

Do whatever you have to do, this is all that counts. Abstinence with drugs and alcohol for me works, it's my recovery program. Please reach out to me if you're struggling or you feel you've got an issue with substances. I'd like to hear about the recovery success stories too. I learned we're not alone when we ask for help. More accurately, I learned I never had to be alone again.

A large part of my day is laughing and being in love with my wife, Michella. She has been unconditionally supportive of me and my ambition to write about recovery, healing, and living life on life's terms. I love, respect, and am inspired by her very much, she gets referenced many times in the book, yet still probably not enough. We have our days when we're both a little grouchy, not very often, it reminds me, these days reminds me we're both humans.

Warning Label

I was recently listening to *Born A Crime* by Trevor Noah, a book I highly recommend. He explained his experiences with young heartbreak and philosophy with girls. It highlighted my missed opportunity to take off pressure and torment from myself as a young man in a small town. Noah's approach was to understand where you fit into the order of things with young boys and girls. People categories start lining up as following even in elementary school: pretty, handsome, charming, stunning, cute, average, funny, smart, meh, asshole, fringe, poor, middle, rich, and a few others.

I felt a little sorry for myself because of my many unknown, unspoken crushes on girls I grew up with that never went anywhere. It would have helped if I ever expressed my crush. When raised in a small school, you know everyone, their family, and even their family that you don't know. It's just a tiny town, way it happens.

In my mind, I was in the smart, funny, fringe, charming, and poor/ middle categories, not in good-looking or smooth but good friends with those who were. I was in a chubby friend-of-the-girl guy category, not asking them to be my girlfriend. This category blows but it can be what you make of it, I went dark and angry versus light and positive. If I'd understood the order and worked with this versus labored over what I wasn't and wouldn't ever have a relationship with them. I couldn't be the natural conduit to the handsome, smoother guys, a missed opportunity.

Life would have been a lot better. I wouldn't have met all the girls and guys from the other towns because that is where I started dating, felt like less risk going outside of the small-town-family. Reflecting it's funny and quite amazing to think about it. When my real feelings and thoughts would come rushing out what when I was drinking, later in high school a couple of embarrassing situations occurred, alcohol-fueled honesty is grossly overrated, and there should be a warning label with it. Ultimately my lesson to share is I cared way too much about what I couldn't control, being good with where my own two feet where wouldn't be helpful then. It's where I'm at today, which is what matters for me and everyone.

What to Expect

You're early into reading my book, I'll leave you alone to draw your own conclusions and thoughts. I want to share a suggestion given to me years ago during my early A.A. meetings. Try to look for similarities, not differences when others share their story. Just consider we're all working through different baggage & experiences, no one is free until you find ways to heal damage or add tools to manage the emotional gaps.

The great thing about this collection of stories, you don't need to start or end in any spot to make sense of them. I hope you're able to identify with someone, or something in the book, that helps. I love being an alcoholic in long-term recovery, it feels like I finally know who I am. Now how about we get healthy together. Keep going, never stop, always keep trying or supporting someone willing to try recovery until happens.

Chapter 2

Our Addiction

THOSE SUFFERING FROM SUBSTANCE USE DISORDER such as myself are sometimes referred to as an addict, an alcoholic, drunk, junkie, and much worse. Note that I use these addict and alcoholic as terms to describe myself interchangeably, the others I don't feel describe people in recovery. I think those terms maintain the status quo for negative stigma about addiction. We all have various opinions on what fits us. I'm respectful of others opinion and what suits them. This book is written using words and tone as I speak. Those suffering from addiction are our daughters, sons, brothers, sisters, parents, partners, friends, and most importantly our fellow human beings. Not everyone who is struggling with a substance use disorder ends up under that a bridge, or on a corner or in front of the convenience store begging. I'm not judging anyone who has been in either of these scenarios or much worse; they're; they're doing all they know trying to survive long enough to either get the next fix or help. I've learned by having talked with hundreds of people conversations with those struggling with substance use, as well my own lived experience, that relief comes in many forms. The difference between using and recovery is the smallest of gray lines more than not. My hope is maybe they survive another day, long enough to find help.

The addiction spectrum is vast and elaborate on depths of how bad it gets before willingness becomes more than the pain you are numbing with substances and behaviors. There are many cases where recovery never happens, and the disease of addiction is fatal. I've known and have friends who collectively lost upwards of 50 people in their life. These friends and family died due to addiction to drugs or alcohol; almost all tried to stop several times.

I've learned and appreciate how different understanding both sides of loss can be. It's always tragic to lose another talented and beautiful person to these cruelties, horrible disease and disorders. In recovery what I've found, and, it's essential is the reminder of how much better and worse it could and has been in life. Those in recovery these lessons are tangible about what life becomes if we relapse or don't. The stakes are the highest, the winning pot of rewarding the biggest only if I don't use again., and a gamble I am sure not ever "planning" on taking. I've seen firsthand where mental health puts the choice of sobriety even further away from someone who needs it. It's hard to comprehend how complex a mental health disorder further strengthens a wall someone can't get over or around to get help. 90% of diagnosed substance use disorder cases have a co-occurring mental health disorder1. This is the reason that for many, only going to 12-step peer group meetings like A.A., N.A. Celebrate Recovery, Smart Recovery, and even Al-anon won't be enough to get their life back. It could take therapy, medication plus a good peer support program to find recovery.

Occasionally a miracle happens, and we somehow find our way out of the darkness to recovery, I've only seen and experience the wonder with a lot of work on myself and giving back to the recovery commu- nity as well those in need no matter whatever community. My story is I surrendered to the fact that I'm an alcoholic and asked for help before I died or accidentally killed someone innocent. The still suffering alco- holic who fight each day trying to survive with sickness, dysfunction and lots of pain are those I must support.

What group is substance-use-disorder is impacting the most? The numbers of deaths and unreported use of alcohol and drugs are skyrock- eting with a much older age group. This signals a public health crisis with addiction is reaching across all age, race, and gender groups. As a reference point, addicts of any kind represent 15% of the U.S. workforce, 20% of the adult U.S. population, and 80% of those diagnosed with a mental health disorder in the United States. These statistics are based on those over the age of 12, anecdotally this is within a year that most in A.A., I've met started using drugs or alcohol.

Note to self, addiction is the most equal opportunity killer that indiscriminately comforts us, right up to the point it doesn't any longer. Addiction never soothes as it did before, it proceeds to quickly take the role of emaciating us emotionally, physically, and spiritually.

Everyone deserves as many chances as it takes to live the best life, we can possibly live, free from addiction. Addicts are some of the smartest, entertaining, and creative people I've ever met. Note that I've met some epic people, you know who you are. I've reiterated a message for support to those who need it, several times throughout the book.

The term enablement is considerably different from support and help. A person's heart might be in the right place, it makes us feel better, but it doesn't help the addict. Please don't enable them, they just require our support, empathy, and love to get better. Don't forget them but work to understand their struggle, keep offering love and availability when they're ready to get better. Share with them that you support them to keep trying to find recovery until it works. I was given more changes than I can remember until it finally happened. Am I able to share concrete evidence why it happened, why I ask for help, no. But sometimes faith has to be just faith.

It is my responsibility to continue to carry this message to the 1 in 5 Americans who will experience bouts with substance use disorder each year.

Alcohol-Related Deaths — An estimated 88,000 people (approximately 62,000 men and 26,000 women) die from alcohol-related causes annually, making alcohol the third leading preventable cause of death in the United States. The first is tobacco, and the second is poor diet and physical inactivity.

In 2014, alcohol-impaired driving fatalities accounted for 9,967 deaths (31 percent of overall driving fatalities).

Chapter 3

Discovery

A S MY LIFE STARTED IN 1969, it began with grief, trauma, love, and racing in a muscle-car on the freeway out of Redwood City, California. I generously admit it's a little weird but couldn't be more poetic based on how my life for the next 41 years went —the twist and turns, discovering how fast you could go before crashing. I finally learned how many times you hit the wall before you die or stop the damage and change your life. I'd like to share how my mind as an alcoholic operates.

In recovery, the memories are coming back to me in a form that I feel involved versus in story form. I had long periods of being lost in the chaos, emotional pain, and darkness. It's amazing how healing and love reveal what's been boxed up in my memories. It's a mix of good and bad memories, I got good at holding on the good ones but living in the bad ones. Addiction is consuming to those with the disorder; as well anyone that has a relationship that touches that person. It is indeed a family disease because it impacts the family (and friends). Addiction occupies one's mind, body, and spirit, it's a whole-person and entire-family disorder.

Upon finding recovery, after asking for help, I've unlocked a life that was more than I'd ever understood could exist. It never occurred to me, I deserved peace, calm, and happiness. It never entered my thoughts that we all deserve these things.

How an alcoholic thinks:

- I don't fit in anywhere.
- What is wrong with me. (statement not a question)
- They deserve that, I don't.

I had all these negative and looping thoughts, lies, and stories that I was telling myself. Another consistent one, "I won't do that again, next time," this was a genuine promise to myself and others. It was defeat from the second it came out of my mouth because I didn't have the capacity to stop using yet.

My addiction turned my lies into my reality, a great example of not being honest with myself, I told myself hundreds of times then drank or used, only 2 drinks. What total bullshit, my disease was telling me I was fine, I had no defenses in place to combat this cycle of destruction.

My inner dialogue for most of my life was so messed up about my ability to consume drugs (alcohol and drugs) until I surrendered my will. The ability to drink quote-unquote like a reasonable person was not possible for me, bless others who honestly figure this out. I'm not one of them until I actively embraced my recovery process. That day when I couldn't hide from myself any longer was the day, a first day that I was ready to ask for help. Only then was I able to put purpose into my thoughts and actions.

40 years I'd felt alone, true or not, it was my reality, then one day I finally didn't feel so alone anymore. It's a weird and surreal transition when it happens. It takes practice to give a shit about yourself and even more practice to believe others, complete strangers care about you and your recovery. Imagine these thoughts looping over and over on replay in someone's mind, mainly all alcoholics experience this.

My message: You're my people, and always will be my tribe. Hang in there today for a few minutes or an hour, do what you can. We all started there and recovered a little bit by little bit, together, you're never alone.

"The grace of God is a wind which is always blowing."

— RAMAKRISHNA

The negative words were all I could hear. It was hopeless, and I was desperate without any hope. My choices were slowly killing me. It came down to me hitting-a-bottom, a point where asking for help was a better option than the pain. I knew my path was starting to narrow, it was heading to death or prison if I continued the same way, same day. Something had driven me to ask someone for help and mean it as if my life depended on it. These actions were going to change my life so significantly. Little did I know; my life really did depend on it. Hopeless, desperate, and a need to vomit were my thoughts when I woke up my first sober morning. I have never taken another drink by the grace of something much bigger than my self-will.

Chapter 4

Living Today

A FRIEND RECENTLY SHARED WITH ME his philosophy about marriage, it was such a brief but powerful conversation about compassion for your partner and yourself. This was one of the bits of wisdom that found me at the right place and right time. I love this when it happens my life.

I'd categorize myself as a little broken, I didn't know how to cope with these cracks in me, thus my love of alcohol, drugs, and emotion changing behavior. I'm not sure if broken is the best word for what recovery has allowed me to restore with my life. Maybe one can't be crushed or broken if one can't be fixed. I say this because I don't need fixing, it's more about being repaired, using things that didn't exist before recovery, I'm a real work in progress. I anticipate changing with time, and more work, more asking for help.

Recovery from alcoholism gave me a life I'd not considered I deserve. It was one life I thought everyone else had, whether real or not, it was my reality right up to the last drink. It's necessary for me to remember this; it's not how things are today, but I balance respecting my past with being present today, working on me.

> *"We meet and come together with those we love to work through our rough edges."*
>
> — MATT KELLEY, AUTHOR

To set up our journey together with my book, my writing style. I tend to use micro-thoughts and broken sentences with an occasion for misplaced words. I'll be candid with you, lovely reader, the story can jump around and likely feel a bit chaotic at points, please I'm humbly asking you to hang in there with me. To quote British food writer, Mary Berry, "It's a bit informal." Ms. Berry's food quote is spot-on my writing style. I bring conversationally, shorter thoughts with an occasional run-on story about my journey of #addiction, healing in #recovery, and lifestyle. Next, my language is a little spicy, not a lot but some, like great Mexican food! My articulations of situations can be colorful and hopefully entertaining like purchasing dented canned goods with no labels. My terminology, it rubs folks, I'd mentioned this a couple of times, setting expectations. I've met with people who've not been fans of the terms I use to describe myself and substance-use disorder (alcoholic, addiction, addict). That's alright; I respectfully chose to use my own words, not to increase stigma, it's how I describe. The various disorders and treatments for co-dependency, anxiety, depression, and other addictions are from the perspective of my lived experience, not being a clinician in this mental health field.

I'm committed to working hard to end stigma with addiction and those experiencing mental health episodes and treating disorders. Part of ending stigma from my vantage point is not fearful of communicating with context and truth about your lived experience. Again, stick with me in the book, how about we agree to work together to see what you identify with in my stories. If not for you, then maybe read for someone you know and care about that is struggling from addiction, trauma, or just life in general.

Yes, I agree on words matter, these are my words and lived experience, and from a place of compassion, healing, and love for my fellow human being, so please keep reading. I'm not out to prove anyone right or wrong, especially clinicians, scientists, or climate change experts— they already have their hands full. We must be in this together, community and connection and smarter approaches to access treatment are how to start winning against this public health crisis.

After years in recovery, sharing and writing about addiction and shame that comes with, I'm finally comfortable describing myself and my journey in my way. Whatever you choose to identify with isn't right or wrong, it's yours, not anybody's decision to make but you. We should hug it out. My timeline shared in the book, I'll be walking back through my recovery and early life to reevaluate and unpack bags of my past and present. Those who acquire this book in a donation box someday at local goodwill or a giveaway bag at an A.A. or N.A. meeting, I hope the book helps, we're the same person.

First Book

My first book *Note to Self: a collection of 99 life lessons* is something I'm very proud to have published in 2015. It's always going to be my first, which makes it unique to me. I'll never write another first book, and thankful to all those who supported me and contributed to that work. Thank you, and I still love and adore you all.

I've been thinking, meditating, and praying about a year about my next book. There were several other book ideas, outlines galore with starts and restarts of writing. In the end, I won't abandon my Note To Self-series, and technically there should be at least two books to be a called a "series." The second book in the series is Sober is Better, A Note To Self. I go deeper into my story, introducing new topics from my experiences. It'll be four years since my first book, wow, so many changes in my life and the world since 2015. Many worlds change we'd never thought possible until they happened.

I've got a new job in the healthcare technology industry to support my writing, and I was looking for a new challenge. It's an excellent group to work, they support my recovery. We focus on software solutions for mental health, substance recovery, public health, vital records, and hopefully corrections at some point. I purchased and sold a house, got a new car because the other one was broken. I've remarried, met and married a great woman. I've also expanded my mid-section and ass by gaining forty-stress pounds from not exercising, I'm working on this as part of my overall health recovery. The time passed since book #1 has put me in a different place on several topics as it relates to what I've shared in my recovery journey.

My hope is I've continued to demonstrate growth in my recovery, enough to help myself and others with my stories. This healing allows me to be more honest and articulate about my thoughts, experiences, and spiritual growth.

Chapter 5

My Early Story

THE PARTY IN RAGED AS I was born in the San Francisco area, a little south in Redwood City, July 1969. This year was also known for the summer of love, the Vietnam war, protesting a lot, walking on the moon, and many drugs consumed to expand one's consciousness. Being born in the middle of this, I feel contributory in some way, no idea how, it just feels like it should. I'm grateful that I was adopted, for my adoption being part of ultimately, who I am today. It was facilitated with what I describe as the best of intentions by my birth mother. She was navigating decisions basically alone of which I'm empathetic, I genuinely respect yet struggle to put myself in her shoes. It feels like it would be a lonely time.

I'd always felt a pull to the west coast, California specifically, long before I'd discovered I was born there. It's interesting how those genetic unknowns could have an impact on us. Mine was a private adoption, very expensive for that point in time as my adoptive parents where hard-working class people from a small town in the middle of Wyoming, a thousand miles away.

> "We must accept finite disappointment, but never lose infinite hope."
>
> — Martin Luther King, Jr.

Private adoption in California with attorneys could be thousands of

31

dollars in 1969, it's not money my new parents had. In fact, $2,000 in 1969 is equivalent to $13,717 in 2019. It's more than their house was worth back then. The adoption was initiated through a relative of my mom, a registered nurse at Sequoia Hospital in Redwood City. It was a higher power, God, whatever the spiritual reference you'd like, was doing what it does best, putting a relative in a path that impacted me the rest of my life.

Much later in life, I was able to learn about the doctor who delivered me, which was an exciting piece of my puzzle I'd not expected to learn about. He had a son who was a doctor at the same hospital, maybe someday I'll get to meet that person. When adopted, with no history, little bits of information are the equivalent of unlocking a new element on the periodic table on individual importance.

> *"Fate, destiny, and luck. Three words to some, three saviors to me. Any adopted child can tell you these words shape the core of our appreciation and embody our sense of vulnerability in the world. I was adopted at birth and I am a living story of fate, destiny and luck."*
>
> — DILLON HENRY, THE DILLON HENRY FOUNDATION

I'll circle back later to the relationships with my biological family—mother, sisters, and father. I've not yet connected with all my immediate biological family at the time of writing this book. An update in early 2019, was an arrival of new consumer DNA test results. These results opened many questions for me to think about and research. This information confirmed what was supposition until the data was there to prove who my biological family was on my father's side. I'm sure not everyone is as excited about this news as I am but to be fair, I have not confirmed anything yet.

My new parents made the trip from Riverton, Wyoming to Redwood City, California—two dramatically different worlds—to pick me up for the long ride to my new home. The new family was very typical, a historically traditional structure in 1969 consisting of a mom and dad, grandparents, uncles and aunts, and many cousins. It was a huge family, 34 great uncles, and aunts, do the math on this big one. The family chapter in Portola Valley, Berkley, and Redwood City were left behind closed but not completely for 33 years. When I departed as an infant, I wasn't addicted to alcohol or drugs yet, then upon return, many years later I was in recovery from the drugs and still actively raging with alcohol.

A new family in Wyoming, another family, left behind, then all sorts of people always around, this was my early years. Having family around was all that I knew. My adoptive family's ancestry was Irish, German, Swedish, and English. Although I'd argue there had to be some NOMAD/gypsy mixed in somewhere based on my experience with them.

One side of the family always was moving, place to place, searching but never settled. They weren't above taking advantage of situations unfairly and entirely living with all gray area in both life and belief systems with people who crossed their path. I still loved them, they included me in the adventures, which I honestly sometimes enjoyed when I was younger.

The other side was mostly stable, considerably more religious and never really moved at all to compare fairly. Life with this side was mainly about the family ranch, raising and running a business that had been around since the early 1900s in the Wind River Valley in Wyoming. A beautiful place with great memories for me as a child. When I compare the two sides, it was a complete contrast of family culture, to say the least. Loved both sides for the same reasons, they included me, adoringly it felt like at times. Both sides of my family knew each other growing up in rural Wyoming. Again, I loved my family for who they are than what they did.

My mother's father was always a John Wayne character to me, he was concerned when mom and dad started dating based on everyone in the family telling me this. Why because he was in trouble often enough, dad was another side of the tracks kid dating a good girl (mom).

Everything I've heard from family; my grandfather respected my dad after mom and dad got married because dad was someone that grandpa couldn't outwork. Simple, old school reason to respect someone. Many years after my grandfather died, I met someone who knew him professionally. They told me a story, one of many they could have said to me about grandfather, they'd added. This guy shared that my grandfather was not a man to be crossed, if he wanted something, he would get it or his way. There was very little to stop him. It is always a trip when your perception is rattled by someone else reality. I'm sure the look on my face confusion and questioning. It's something I'd never heard. I do wish I'd known all my grandparents better if I were in recovery back then and an adult, I would appreciate very different conversations with them.

One might have formed options at this point that my life wasn't hard or traumatic. I questioned this more than anyone else ever will. My challenge and trauma were that, mine. I've only a few incidents as something tangible that happened. At this point my problem of feeling like I don't fit into any group was in part due to such a large family; I got lost in the crowd. It's a grand theory but I've thought about this, and I don't feel this to be the case. Additional context, it doesn't make sense because we never lived around family past my age of 4. I would have liked it too be around. We moved away from everyone when I was young. I've felt my issues were centered around detachment, utterly alone in a crowd goes all the way back to my adoption. This trauma revived and relived again when I was four.

When I left California, that was all I knew, all two days. I was relocating my life with albeit loving people, I had no connection to them personally, or physically because I'd only know my biological mother's womb to that point.

This trauma was buried in my subconscious, with the adoptive birth experience where my life changed, two days old and unknowing. A move to Nebraska left me feeling more alone than ever. For reasons, I didn't understand until 40 years later. Part of the reason I support and an open to many types of therapies, support groups, and treatments is my personal experience healing traumas of the past. Due to this break-through about the unknown detachments in my background, I highly support trying breathwork meditation.

The summer of 1969 is where my addiction all started because I was born, an obvious point but with a propensity of substance use disorder, depression, and anxiety raging in my genetics, I was playing against a stacked deck. I'm surprised I wasn't given formula in a pint glass—fast track the inevitable, right, just kidding that would've been weird with an infant in a pub, drinking milk with a little Irish whiskey out of the pint. Let's be honest, it's likely not the first time though.

I'm at complete peace with my history to this point. It's my story, I get the opportunity to share these experiences in a way to help others heal and find recovery. Some might say it would have been nice to know that addiction was prevalent in my birth family. 20/20 hindsight knowing my genetic makeup, places of origin, I likely wouldn't have changed much. We'll never know so why spend much time thinking about it. I was afforded lots of experiences on my path, before and after addiction recovery.

Part of recovery was learning how not to regret changing the past nor controlling the future, which isn't possible even if I wanted to be a future controller. Recovery has taught me life skills one of which is living in the present, the now. The second half of life is about me helping others with what I've learned to help myself. How I saved my life, or my life was saved could help someone else.

I left the hospital on that hot August day with my newly acquired parents. (Thank you for wanting me to be part of your family, I'm not sure I'd ever expressed that. I hope you knew how much I appreciated and loved you.)

My exit from the Northern Cali was in a 1969 Dodge Super Bee. I'm painting the picture of the movie like soundtrack playing, a blue sports car fading out of focus as they depart, new adventures ahead for the trio

headed to Wyoming. A dodge super bee, people, one of the most herald-
ed of a limited product muscle car in the late '60s and early 70s. I'm
excited about it apparently.

I rolled out of the future Silicon Valley in my new parent's super-
cool, classic muscle car, racing out of the valley—a dramatic yet appro-
priate description from my vantage point. It's no wonder I liked speed so
much, note both miles-per-hour and drug slang. We roared out of there
through the hills to the first set of many mountains; it was hotter than
hell itself that day. It was unseasonably warm when we left that early
part of August, it was fun to look this up to fact-check the temperate in
Redwood City in August 1969. The internet is great.

Traveling through California, Nevada, Utah, and ultimately home
to central Wyoming, it's a scenic drive if you're not 2 days old. No one
could have known these first few days would impact the rest of my life
so significantly, to this very day. This hot and winding travel so early in
my life, unscientifically I attribute for my child and adult severe motion
sickness.

Growing up, I had a bus driver nicknamed ZoomZoom, this because
he drove like a bat out of hell plus it was part of his name (thanks Dave).
I would vomit from being bus-sick every single day in 1st grade, it was
horrible. Mom figured out a plan, she exchanges me part way on the
daily bus trip before I'd get sick. Thanks, mom! This did workout pretty
well, I know I wasn't puking on the bus daily. My mom was a professional bus driver for 20 years, I've always had and always will be proud
of Donna (my mom). I wasn't a fan of ZoomZoom's driving but he was
good history teacher.

Back to me, being thrashed around moving with no control over
the temperature, meaning it was broiling, feels like a situation that
might cause some type of physical trauma to an infant. The best part of
knowing I can't handle these types of motions, I saved a fortune in the
roller coaster and boat rides in my lifetime. One of the miracles in my
life is the invention and introduction of Dramamine to my life, wow. It

was beautiful and improved the quality of my life when I was moving in unknown directions quickly, I could see the ocean, mountains, dodgy little planes but still no roller coasters.

I traveled from sea-level to 7694 feet in the mountains in only a couple of days, that is a lot of change for me as a newborn who physically is displaced from the apartment, I'd been residing for nine months. My parents had zero information on what was happening to me, way back then it's not they could google baby travel trauma to help manage the trip for me. The world in 1969 has no idea, no information, and no access to help with all the issues being experienced by an adopted infant.

> *"Self-hatred and hopelessness stay with you like a shadow."*
>
> — Unknown

My early childhood was surrounded by family and more cousins around than I could count, although just not that high. They'd come and play, and we'd get into little-kid trouble, what I call usual stuff. Due to my alleged gypsy blood of my adopted family in addition to a dose of wild-wild-west (Wyoming) culture, it was invariably an adventure. I see where my dad got it from. There wasn't really anything off the table when the family got together.

We had several family members who are straight-up grifters, a set complete opportunist in their dealings with people, family or not. You must watch your step and wallet around them, not literally but a little bit, this comes out several times in my story. Our getting into trouble wasn't a novelty so much as it was of a legacy. This was passed down through the generations from both of my families, who knew I could leverage both sides of the equation (environmental and genetic).

Wyoming family, I didn't stand a chance, I was going to push the limits of honesty, and genetically I was also wired for the path of least resistance in life. Looking back, I'm somewhat horrified at the little and big things we got away with. We were basically criminals that didn't think it was that big of a deal, who was it really hurting, well not us anyway. I can't change it, so I work to laugh at what I called victimless crimes back then. To make living amends, I go out of my way to do the right thing, whether it feels good or not, doesn't matter. I also question others about the right thing to do, unapologetically. This to continue to work to make up for all the bad things in the past.

My dad conveyed his philosophy of a good time, and I quote, "It wasn't much of a Saturday night unless a fight broke out." This was how he grew up, his normal was completely opposite of what I knew. Occasionally, I'd think I might be a fighter, tougher than I was. I'm laughing as I type, those times was usually wasted on something or lots of somethings. It never really worked out well. I just don't have enough "mean" in me UNLESS pushed, then some level of terrifying comes out from somewhere. I can only suppose why he didn't drive me to be more of a fighter. Maybe he didn't like it as much as he conveyed in his stories. It could be he recognized I was talker and thinker and didn't force his growing up kicking ass whenever the change presented it's on me to continue.

Dad died several years ago, so it's another question mark to be left alone. LeRoy (dad) was the toughest individual I've ever met in my life. I literally saw multiple grown men, tremble and cower when dad confronted them about their actions toward one our family. He was quite the artist and creative but never really allowed himself to explore this side of his personality, I feel the world missed out here. My mom was also tough albeit differently than my dad, sure mom has never been in a fight in her life. She possesses intestinal fortitude and resilient toughness like her parents. Raised on a ranch with cold weather and hard work, she can handle anything and did. Mom supported and persevered with my dad for over 50 years, thanks to being tough and remembered why she fell in love with him. I talk about how he changed later. Candidly, I questioned why she stayed with him for many years, then I made peace with I didn't have all the information, just my side of this. I let the question go, it was not mine to answer.

I will share three great examples of the family shenanigans, people made happen. My cousins and I around age seven decided we were going to mud wrestle, it seems like a very well thought out decision. We came up with a plan, part of which was orchestrated conveniently when the adults were not paying attention or not home, I don't recall. We dug a massive hole behind my uncle and aunt's trailer in their backyard, I remember it being bigger than probably was, but it was a crater. Then proceed to fill it with water, a lot of water when it's coming out of a tiny green garden hose. It took what felt like forever to fill that damn hole, which I was never worried someone would catch us. This proves I didn't feel we were doing anything wrong.

Once the crater was full, OMGoodness we proceeded to get all sorts of filthy, covered in mud, head to toe, every crack and crevasse was filled when done. It was as exciting as MMA of today in the "pit", forty years ago. It was exciting and fun, and it never crossed anyone's mind how much trouble we'd made for ourselves. I still don't know why our parents were so mad, well, other than the large hole in the yard and children entombed in mud.

In the scheme of things, they were "sweating the small stuff" as the author, Richard Carlson explains in his books. Their reaction seemed unreasonable at that time, but I'm not sure it was reasonable to them, even to this day. The net result was harmless fun with no laws being broken, and no one injured. We got scolded and then hosed down outside with cold water, mainly because we were covered in mud, it would have trashed the house. I don't remember my parents saying too much after the fact, I was guest visiting, it was my vacation, I'm exempt from true punishment, it's a rule. Yes, that's right, the good boy got no punishment, I can remember anyway.

An epic tale shared with me 50 times growing up, that stuck with me. My German and Irish side of the family who I categorize as the gypsies in their actions and decisions in life.

A relative of my dad, an uncle, drove into the yard of a country house of a family gathering—Thanksgiving or Easter. There were 40 family members there cooking, drinking, and being raucous, a typical family event. He shared his thoughts, mistakenly about how he hated his car, complaining it was just plain worthless. He didn't like all the problems with it, and then made a statement to the effect, "I wish it would just fall apart, I'd just get a new one." This was a loose interpretation of what story I was told, but it's close.

My dad witnessed this first hand, he said it was a mob mentality after the uncle shared his wishes. The festive group of relatives dropped everything in the house, picked up anything they could carry, heading outside. The make their way directly to the car, beating the shocked uncle's vehicle into a pile of undrivable scrap metal. Dad shared he was in shock, they used shovels, wrenches, and fence posts. The uncle with surprise in his voice, ask why did they do that? He received a simple response: "Because you asked us too." My dad said this wasn't that unique from this crew, this type of thing kept these family of hooligans entertained. Oh, my family is entertaining if nothing else.

My cousin when in town visiting us, we'd go weekly the cow sale in the biggest city in our area, Kearney Nebraska. Many have no idea what I'm talking about, cow sale, what? In the rural areas of the country at least where I was raised there were auction houses that you'd buy and sell animals (cattle, sheep, pigs, horses, chickens, ducks). These animals are in the food chain, not horses-we hope, but all else at some point will likely be slaughtered for consumption by humans or other animals (dog and cat food). I'm both generalizing and simplifying to keep it brief. What is real is if you purchase meat in a pretty package from a grocery store for the game day barbecue, this could be where it came from at some point in the process. I've worked end-to-end, assist a mother cow in giving birth to a gorgeous calf all the way to the packing plant where the slaughter and packaging happened. I've since made a choice to eat less meat, which makes my meat processing experience unique for almost all veggies and vegans.

It was a big deal at the sale to get a bottle of pop, usually grape and maybe some sweets the cow sale. I've converted and do use soda versus pop, I know everyone was wondering about this. Yes, after years in the southeast and living west coast in the U.S., I've changed, I use the term but rarely drink it. When your seven and bored shitless, as my dad used to say, we're always on the lookout for some excitement. My cousin and I were hustlers, we'd go pick up the non-returned bottles to the cafe' and the .10 deposit back, made enough to cover the cost of our sweets. Occasionally some other little child scavengers would move in on our turf, usually not.

One day we saw this gigantic stack of returned pop bottles behind the cafe that was already picked up and returned for the .10 cent. This presented an incredible opportunity to scale our operation, less work more bottles. The apparent issue was they'd already been exchanged for the deposit fee. We knew this was sketchy, but it didn't occur how wrong it was at the time. The scam-we'd grab as many bottles from the stack as our little arms could carry. Then we present for cold hard little kid cash. It was quite the racket, we kept doing it until we got caught. Busted cold. It was my first time I was caught breaking the law. We got off with a warning, stern ass-chewing by someone, I was so scared I don't remember.

My life-my gypsy grandfather was impressed with our racket, he felt they (corporation) had plenty of money. He suggested we try it again in a couple of weeks when they wouldn't recognize us, straight-up lousy influence at times like this one. These were some of my early memories of receiving praise for being a go-getter, a real Enron entrepreneur.

The drinking got more frequent right in parallel with my poor decision making in this area, more bar fights and alleged stealing of lots of things, too numbers to remember. There was gambling, selling alcohol and other stuff in some of my mostly blurry times with and without my family around during the early years. I don't blame the family for my decisions. These were considerably more serious than the innocent mud wrestling. A key point we learned back then was that not getting caught was critical to stay off the radar of everyone especially anyone legal. Nonetheless, there were good memories and experiences, not good for improving society but non-violent mischievous behaviors.

In recovery, today, I've made many amends for the indiscretions. I know these caused problems for others just trying to live their life. I'm not proud also not embarrassed about it. It was in the past, a long time ago, I was ill-equipped to make good decisions and cope with about anything back then. I was trying to change my feelings, in all the unhealthy ways I could find. I was seeking a type of attention that ended up being accomplished by using drugs and alcohol.

Chapter 6

Next Moves

I DON'T REMEMBER FEELING THAT OUT of place or unsettled at age four. This was about the time we moved from Wyoming to Nebraska, away from everyone I'd known my entire life in Wyoming. This was my first move since being separated at birth from my biological mother in California as part of my adoption. This point is essential as I feel it was the beginning of 35 years of feeling out of place, searching for an attachment to anything. I was reliving the trauma again from being adopted, a detachment and separation came right to the surface with nowhere to go, that's my theory.

Because I was older this time, I had more capacity to remember how confusing and unsettled the change was for me. After moving, we settled, and I remained in Sumner, Nebraska for 13 years. I was there until I graduated high school, with an occasional move back when I took a semester off university. Honestly, I didn't come home much because my father and I were not getting along. My drinking and drugs didn't help me getting healthier with any relationships currently. These experiences with this kind of trauma were gained at 48 hours and four years old, removed from safety, at least unconsciously. It set into motion behavioral patterns for a lifetime. The relocation caused some damage, reliving an adoption-trauma unbeknownst to anyone until 40 years later.

My parents or any professional back then would have had any idea that my separation would end up impacting me, significantly in my life.

If they would have been told, I feel they would have tried to help and worked to understand. My mom would have, and maybe dad would have come around later, my dad was dealing with his own recurring issues from growing up in a volatile environment plus combat service in Vietnam.

The change in life was more visible this time, I'd developed attachments and belief system to compare my old life and new life on this move.

Note, not everyone who gets adopted is impacted by the separation at the birth the same way. The research supports a significant correlation between adoption and considerably higher addiction cases, much like those who've experienced a trauma of some form. This separation was a trauma.

I've found as I reflect and experience therapy work to understand what are the underlying elements of my behaviors, I was off and running toward addiction as young as age four. The momentum was fueled by this void caused by detachments. I wanted desperately not to feel this, but it was there my entire life. Based on what happened in the years directly following the move and many years after I believe my theory to be correct.

The act of moving away from my family, the group of people most familiar to me impacted my life in ways that no one understood. By the way, throughout my recovery and writing, I focus on forgiveness, of myself and others. I have worked to not harbor or hold on to resentments from the past. The benefit of doing the work in recovery is figuring out how to let the bitterness and resentments go. It feels like with practice this becomes easier. I don't blame anyone for anything in my life; I hold myself accountable for my part.

The move for my family was what my parents felt was best for us then. A central part of the recovery process, it helped me reconcile the feelings that it was anyone else's fault, I don't feel the need to do that any longer. I survived and have made my own decisions for many years, many good, many bad choices leading to finding a way out of the dark and relentless turmoil.

There is trauma experienced such as physical and sexual assault and abuse that it's NOT THE FAULT of the victim. Recovering from trauma isn't about placing fault with me/you. The title "family" doesn't mean you're required to have a relationship with those who hurt you. It seems to much the norm that it's easier for other, family, friends, and society to default to uneducated advice about forgiveness. What I hear isn't forgiveness, I interpret this advice to be more forgetness. Forgetting about trauma, please don't do this, do the opposite. Ask for help, get help, do whatever you need to do for you, self-care first, live your life and life, not under self-imposed shame prison. Again, please ask for help. This approach will hopefully provide a path for the individual suffering, out of the dee into shame and guilt.

The trauma I reference and address in the books I've written are related to emotional volatility, detachment, and control, we have different situations with some of the same outcomes which impact our lives. I feel compassion and empathy for those who have experienced trauma, it feels like you've no control. It's like you are suspended with no ability to move any direction.

Everyone has the right to process their feelings about their experiences their own way, taking back control of their life. Many who've dealt with emotions, they're working their own healing and solutions, it's from a different point of view from where I am coming from in my experience.

Best Effort

While growing up, my father was committed to not moving us around, keep us in the same school and place to live, stability to him. He'd grown up being unable to settle into a home for long. He and his brothers grew up in a what I'd call a nomadic lifestyle with too many moves to remember and count. I feel it impacted him and his family in significant ways their entire lives.

He swore his family wouldn't do that, so we didn't, he was one to lock into something, and that was that. Not moving around all my childhood feels like it happened for the right reasons, but I'm not this version of stability helped or damaged. I hear quite often those who've experienced trauma when you, especially those in recovery from substance use don't remember a lot from my childhood. I am referencing a lot less than the average. My theory is the memory lapses were a coping mechanism. It's how I dealt with feeling so bad for so long, a form of my detaching. What I do remember are some good things and lots of chaotic things, which overall felt like most of the time for me.

I had no clue what to do with most of my emotions as a kid, so one of my coping mechanisms was losing myself in books and my own stories; my imagination kept me feeling safe. It was something I could control, it felt like one of the few things. It was a survival technique that many children use, I see it as one of the healthier options. This pretending helped me from being a complete emotional disaster as a kid but didn't lend itself to a wealth of memories. I was immersed in my architected story, a distorted reality, not real or actual experiences. It's hard to sort out so many years later.

There is so much I don't recall happening, not just events, or months, it was lost years. One thing I started to remember was a lot of fighting, frustration, and impatience from those around me at home, school, and work when I get older. I remember my dad either cracking a joke or enraged about something; no one ever knew who was going to show up in any situation. It set a pattern with me and the rest of the family, which ended up being a journey of co-dependence, control, and manipulation. We all didn't know what healthy communication and permission to feel anything honestly. This learned behavior of avoiding confrontation set the stage for future avoiding of conflict when I didn't know how to process the feelings.

As I'm doing trauma research and learning more about therapies, I've read and discussed my father quite a lot. I feel that dad was a good guy at the core, he was a traumatized person, transferred to his immediate family. It just happened we were in his chaos generated from his upbringing but more from combat experience in Vietnam. He didn't know how to process what he was feeling about his experience that I can't imagine in Vietnam. With no healthy way to express this, it came out as frustration and anger. He rarely talked about it, only when I was going to basic training for the Army National Guard did, he open about his experience briefly.

Dad had already died when I put the pieces together about why he'd acted so anger, treated our family the way he did for so many years, sadly we can't talk about. This situation inspired and drives me to help others find this information sooner, then they'll be able to talk about it with those who they need help.

I'm sure each member of the family has a different version of the shared experiences that we had. I'm sharing not in judgment of anyone in my family, it's my experience, what I remember, and my path which felt bumpy for a long time. We all went different ways and had different processes to heal from simple and complex experiences and trauma in the past. There will be disagreement with the people involved with parts of my story, but these are based on my memories and interpretation. Others will be correct in their version of certain events, that makes sense because it's what they remember, I'm okay about that. It's alright if we don't all agree on everything; when do families ever agree on everything.

Chapter 7

Farm Crisis

M Y MOM, FOR ME, WAS THE foundation of the family; it was her of my two parents that I spent the most time. My dad was away working or at home working. It's what he could control the most, it kept him busy, it's what he knew to do. Mom always has been and remains to this day an example to many what being kind and loving each day looks like. Many years later, well into adulthood, very recent to writing this book, Mom and I visited about a few things with my childhood. I understand now that she was coping with unexpected personality changes with my dad starting after he returned from his Vietnam service. This, in my opinion, could center around undiagnosed Post Traumatic Stress (PTS). Not being a professional in the psychology field I'm not diagnosing, I'm just observing with some lived experience and research, that's it. Years after he died, I more fully understand that he didn't know why he was mad so often for most of his life after being in combat.

Adding to this stress was enduring owning a family farm and keeping it afloat in one of the nation's most severe financial downturns of the last 100 years for the rural communities in the 1980s, second only to the Great Depression's impact on farm and ranch families. I believe mom did the best she could, and so did my father with was they had to work with at that time. It wasn't for lack of effort, no one I know worked harder than my parents.

The farm crisis in the 1980s was a crystal ball into many elements and events experienced with the 2008 economic collapse, bad money underneath volatile revenue. It was startling to me to see the similarities and differences. I was very engaged in the turmoil this time as an adult, and a small business owner. The farm crisis didn't have massive bailout assistance from the federal government, so that was different. I'm not agreeing or disagreeing, staying in my lane on this. As I reflect on growing up from a perspective of years more experience, I appreciate with new found respect what my parents and others in farm country endured.

My entrepreneurial nature likely comes genetics and environment, my family always owned their own businesses and worked for 3rd parties. I've owned several small companies over the years, many during the time I was not sober. This part of the story heightened the ebbs and flows of my personal and family's financial insecurity, but we figured out a way to survive. Much like life, I've hung on too long to bad decisions several times, my ego and pride have fueled these decisions. In recovery, these are all areas I work on new skills in how I process information, emotions, and the next most fabulous idea that pops into my head.

My Dad's temper I remember becoming more a part of his regular personality; this was exacerbated by working 18 hours a day. Underlying these issues, he was experiencing chronic pain from a previous work injury in the oil fields, and not until many years later was it confirmed his exposure to "Agent Orange" in Vietnam impact his health. He possessed limited skills to communicate about stress and his feelings of fear about the farm failing, and likely what he would have considered his personal failing. This was his experience and trauma combined with a generational norm of not expressing emotions about fear, weakness, and vulnerability. This only made things worse, of course.

He and Mom were trying to make enough money for a family to survive on, and my sister and I didn't know much about how bad things got. My family lived on the edge of insolvency for several years, me none the wiser. One of the reasons the farm survived is because my parents were utterly self-sufficient, always used worn-out farm equipment, and didn't purchase anything new if my dad could build or salvage it from somewhere. This truly saved them. It was the late '70s and '80s where you had families losing everything to bankruptcy. It was just like you might have seen in the movies or read about except it was considerably more painful, and a soul-crushing farm and family crisis.

I saw several families I knew my entire life have the bank they owed a considerable amount of money—much more than possible to pay back. Interest rates skyrocketed, crop and livestock prices dropped, it wasn't possible to repay the loans at the interest rate owed—They lost their farms, businesses, and life's works.

The bank auctioned off, one bid at a time everything that family worked for generations to build. It was scary, stressful, and heartbreaking not only to see this happening but also to have that as a real possibility for my family. It would have taken just one lousy crop or livestock selling season to bankrupt families, and ours was not an exception. I didn't realize any of this as a kid; I just knew my parents were stressed, especially my dad, but had no idea the severity of the situation. Good or bad I feel we were isolated from the harsh economic reality being lived with.

Chapter 8

Poor Folks

I WOULD SAY WE WERE CONSIDERED average-poor; everything earned went into keeping the farm operating. Nearly all food and meat we consumed was raised on the farm, so it didn't seem like we were that poor. Almost everyone was working class that lived in our area, so no one had a lot of extra money. This commonality seemed to even things out for a while on my understanding of our economic standing and security in rural Nebraska. It helped me not be resentful about not having more expensive, name brand things. They were silly thoughts now when I think about them in comparison to what is important in my life (health, sobriety, serenity) but that was how I felt back then.

Around seven years old, I started feeling out of place with everything, mostly with myself but was out of sync with the world around me. I'd gained some weight about that time and feeling fat as compared to those around me. This started impacting my identity, image, and self-worth. It felt like I was not like everyone else, always not living up to a standard in my own mind. A belief that stuck with me for many years.

This struggle with identity also began to happen about the time I was told about being adopted, which in hindsight, might have exacerbated that feeling of being different. I'm not sure about this, could be a coincidence. The constant awareness of not fitting in was more significant than just being at an awkward age.

At home from my perspective my younger sister and I started to

behave in a way to avoid making my dad angry, avoiding conflict at all
cost. I learned this was the more comfortable, softer way to manage and
live our daily lives. My everyday experience was to avoid confrontation,
burying how I felt, a technique adopted to change my reality into something manageable. That's how I started to explore how to control people,
which helped manage the chaos I was feeling. It felt like this every single
day, and nothing seems to make made sense.

I found a way to control my life by manipulating myself and others
with partial information, selected exaggerations, and outright lying.
Years into recovery, I refer to this time as my learning to step, dance and
run away from the truth, conflict, feelings, and anything else remaining.
It became a complete coping strategy for me for the next few youthful
years until I found alcohol.

As I learned about manipulation, humor, avoidance, selective truths,
colorful language, anger, and a fear to speak what was on my mind. This
emotional mess I was becoming included unconditional love from my
mom and sister. Conflict and contrast were just part of my life. I can
remember being in 1st or 2nd grade in Eddyville, Nebraska, someone
who shall remain nameless because I can't remember who told the
teacher I was using bad language. I got detention, oh I was fucking mad
at this accusation.

It was true, no doubt, it was the communication I was used to
hearing from my dad and grandfather, not my mom. I'd think it was also
how I protected myself from what I was feeling back then. No hard feelings person who dropped the dime on me, I probably need a timeout for
some reason.

> "The rage wasn't at our family; it was about humanity he
> lost in what he was forced to do and see in Vietnam. He
> raged with this most of his life."
>
> — ME

I hope that in my father's death, he has absolute peace with what he was carrying for so long in life. I love you Dad.

I remember a lot of fighting, by one set of grandparents, by my father, uncles, and aunts, and a few other poor souls not in the family, who made the mistake of crossing Dad's path. He possessed the ability to scare the shit out of grown adult men who considered themselves bullies. It was one of the things I admired about my father, he wasn't scared of other people. There was something that kicked in when confrontation presented itself. I never wondered if he was in a situation that he couldn't defend himself, not once. This was something I'd admired and feared about him.

I'm not sure if it was stress from work or the isolation of rural life combined with his Vietnam experience that pushed him to breakpoints. I don't know, and we'll never know. All those years of back problems because you were active as a bull and lifted too much by yourself, heart issues from genetics, and more health issues from working in uranium mines, or exposure to Agent Orange in Vietnam, the list seem quite lengthy of what contributed to what was wrong. I didn't feel dad presented himself as a victim ever, that I can remember. He appeared to take action about and fix things with everything but his emotions. His pain ended quickly, he died in June 2014 at the age of 71.

My dad had such a good sense of humor, cracked himself and most everyone he met up; I know this is likely where I'd got my sense of humor. When I was younger, he'd become livid just a breath after laughing about something. His day was spent being mad, and that was pretty much what I remember growing up more than his guttural laughter and kidding around with my mom. His conflict was with himself, but we shared in this as a family. Despite all this, he did his best, and I miss him.

Liking Whiskey

My inner dialogue with myself about my feelings was already starting to be a constant companion of mine even at a young age, but no outer voice had emerged yet. I remember around six was the first time I took a drink of alcohol, it was a beer of some kind. It tasted horrible, but I liked being included with the adults. The beer, then a whiskey sour, lots of sour; I was an overachiever at drinking even back then by drinking both early and as often as I could con my way into tasting it. It started young, me trying to drink like the adults, fit in. I'm sure I negotiated or snuck a way to try both, many times and that was the start of my alcohol as a solution. I was probably drinking with my Uncles way more times than they realize or remember.

Growing up as a future addict/alcoholic with no mindfulness made me always chasing something outside of myself, something better, and finding anything but what was going on in my head. I'd do anything not to be left alone with my thoughts.

Life on the farm was a normal rural life in the middle of Nebraska. Most worked 10-12 hours a day when not in school, and the work was a little dangerous. There were days we got excused from school to work, help with a harvest or working cattle. I hated those days because it felt like I was missing out on something at school. My attitude made the day worse and longer. The work and the day were harder because of the chaos also going on in my head.

I knew lots of people who got severe injuries, even killed growing up—my parents and grandfathers. It was and still is part of life on the farm, dangerous work. You're likely going to get hurt, get scars to carry around, and maybe get killed a real possibility. One of my memories was my grandfather getting most of his thumb cut off by a 20-foot belt running equipment to grind corn into corn meal. It was a dangerous beast of a machine by anyone's standards. My mom was burned, dad broke ribs, and my grandfather was killed in an accident.

It's an isolated existence on the farm, so doing activities such as sports and 4-H were important for socializing off the farm with non-family and other human beings. For those who don't know, the program of 4-H is America's largest youth development organization—empowering nearly six million young people across the U.S. with the skills to lead for a lifetime. You grow and show animals and do lots of other things in competitions, much like the Westminster Kennel Club Dog Show minus all the fancy stuff like tv-cameras'.

One of the 4-H programs was a horse judging competition much like a baking competition on TV, but you don't eat the horses. I competitively judged horses one-time, yes, one-time. I possessed zero knowledge about what made for a championship horse or not. I'd been approached by a leader in the county organization about judging, which felt nice to be asked to join the team. But my reason for being there was to meet and hang out with a girl named Amy from a bigger town, had a crush on her. I'd later learned that was a poor reason to be in a horse judging competition. I remember a smart and pretty young woman with wealthy parents. For the record, I didn't care about the affluent part; it wasn't her money to spend on me, come on.

To his credit, my dad did in his way warn me that I didn't know a damn thing about judging horses. No, that's what he told me correctly, "you don't know a damn thing about judging horses." I was defensive about his brash observation, today I'm in complete agreement. How time changes one's perspective and pride.

My plan quickly went up in flames because the girl I wanted to hang out with was not only good, she was one of the best in the state at judging horses. I sucked, shouldn't have been there. Judging horses is especially hard when you know nothing. She was excited about winning the competition, all competitions as she was very successful at judging horses and yes, I was on her team.

We didn't win that day; she rightfully wasn't impressed. I didn't follow up with her about anything after that experience. It was one of the fake-it-until-you-make-it moments that I was trying to fit into a group and feel normal. This one didn't work out well. It was painful to fake a skill, so I'd suggest not trying it.

Again, isolation even today is an issue with agricultural communities as demonstrated by the rural mental health crisis. There is a high occurrence of depression, various anxiety disorders, and substance misuse. The extreme lack of services to address the mental health demand in rural areas will only continue to get worse until more funding is made available and technology innovations such as telehealth become a standard extension with available primary care (hospitals). Primary care because less-populated areas tend to have at a minimum these facilities.

Resources

https://www.ruralhealthinfo.org/topics/mental-health
SAMHSA's National Helpline
Phone: 800-662-4357
Hours: 24/7

NCADD Hope Line
Phone: 800-622-2255
Hours: 24/7

National Suicide Prevention Lifeline
Phone: 800-273-8255
Hours: 24/7

The Trevor Lifeline (LGBTQ+)
Phone: 866-488-7386
Hours: 24/7

U.S. Department of Veterans Affairs Veterans Crisis Line
Phone: 800-273-8255
Hours: 24/7

National Domestic Violence Hotline
Phone: 800-799-7233
Hours: 24/7

Chapter 9

Bio + Adopted

B ACK TO THE START. I WAS adopted about the same as my younger sister. It was just the two of us, and we were three years apart. It was enough years that we didn't do a lot together. She was quiet and did her own thing. I remember being in my world, not at all present, even all the way back then. At nine I was figuring out how to feel better, how to escape what felt like a chaotic life already. Not much of a brother or the right person to be around when I was obsessing about things such as how much I hated everything from living on a farm to well, life in general.

I'm sorry about this for my sister; I wished I was there more for her and me both back then. I apologize, sis, I think I did for all the stuff, but in case I didn't. It wasn't all bad. We did have some adventures, chasing around the farm with a pack of greyhound and Irish wolfhounds that my parents raised to hunt. Traipsing all over pastures looking for whatever treasures you think you're going to find as kids.

My sister was big into riding, she liked riding horses, and I did not. I loved motorcycles and betting on horses when I got older. We'll save the betting on horses for my next book. The horses and I didn't get along, my guess is they sense my uneasiness, and it makes them jumpy and nervous, but we just had restless horses.

I've recently been introduced to a group of people who do networking and personal development for veterans using horses. The horses can sense the emotions of those working with them, it helps calm. Psychology Today, explained the being in the barn grooming, feeding, and otherwise caring for horses reduces stress, lowers blood pressure, and improves overall health. Yet, it is the companionship with equine partners that is the foundation of growth in relationship to these animals. Being with horses is "therapy."

I'm thankful and interested to learn more about the effects of being with horses. My dad was, and my sister is a huge horse fan. They loved them, and it could have provided therapeutic relief for dad whether he knew it or not. Mom liked horses but not as much as those two.

We didn't have much family close to where I grew up, distant cousins, who were lovely but older than my sister and me. They were cool, older, take-no-crap kind of farm people, they were robust personalities. They all worked hard, some played harder than others, but overall, they were an excellent small extended family. We had grandparents in the area, four miles away. It's my gypsy side of the family; I couldn't help but love them, but it was where I saw the examples of yelling as a solution for everything and consistent unhappiness.

One was full Irish, equipped with red hair and fiery temper, and the other was full German, impatient, and a little dodgy occasionally. They would fight like nothing I'd seen growing up. It was loud, ruthless, not physical, and not any help calming down my own emotional upheaval. It ended up being more of the chaos; I loved my grandparents because they spent time with me growing up, my closest family but wow they did fight a lot.

My grandfather and I had a thing, he always picked me to drive his new car first. He didn't need nor could he afford the new car, but he chose me to drive it first. For many years this happened without me having a driver's license because I was ten years old. Grandpa wasn't one to think twice about laws or rules like most people would consider, I witnessed this first hand more times than I can possibly remember.

I was his partner playing pinochle, a card game. On the farm, you play games to pass the time with family and friends. Anyway, we sucked at winning any of the games we played, but we went big when we lost. We'd be trying game after game, cheating when possible to win. I attribute my strategic thinking to learning this card game before I was seven. Another reason I looked past all the issues was that I was with the family hanging out. This was letting me part of the group afforded them more than a reasonable amount of clemency on the poor behavior, I got to hang with the adults. It was excellent at that age.

My parents worked a lot; it was just what you do when you're on a farm. I grew up on a ranch more than a farm for the record, everything we raised on the farm part was used on the ranch part for the animals. They worked steadily, too many 100-hour weeks to count, almost worked themselves into the grave at times. I owe my work ethic to them, as much as I honestly don't care for doing farm work, I know how to do it, not a fan of doing it.

My sister was good at it though, she liked the farm. Really good at milking the cows, right sis? She'd love to tell you that story of my manipulation to get her to do my chores.

Negotiation skills started developing from trying to get out of doing work on the farm. It's a different lifestyle caring and killing animals. In recovery, I've moved to mostly a plant-based lifestyle, not entirely but close. The choice was driven by more health than moral reasons, but still, it's hard to imagine doing what we did to process animals into eatable meat growing up.

Recovery from alcoholism changed more than just not drinking anymore. It turns your entire life into something different, healing physically, emotionally, and spiritually with more awareness and progression. Referencing and talking about killing animals is a little surreal, basically a different life. My parents were more humane and cared about the animals, but ironically that was before we ate or sold them for food. The feels not very compassionate, but it's part of the past, one more contraction to wrestle.

It was what life was about then. My hope is this makes sense to the veggies, vegans, and planters who are supporting someone in recovery or recovering themselves. Peace, people, peace!

Chapter 10

Age Ten

A T TEN YEARS OLD, I WAS above average at sports and good in school; I started to feel better about fitting in because I learned fast. Most things than not came naturally to me. I wasn't a fan of standing out nor did I like asking for help with much, so I rarely did. Some of the toughest times for me were being dismissed when I didn't understand something, then being berated when I was asking questions about the project. The lack of patience and following anger about my lack of ability can still be a trigger for me, even 40 years later. These early experiences really inset strong patterns, which take a lot of work to change. I'm still working on it. These experiences as a kid can leave an imprint that doesn't go away; it just sits in the background until reactivated to the surface.

My quick learning and lying about not understanding kept me from being noticed when doing anything with a group. My goal was not being seen. I was always formulating emotional control and manipulation plans with everyone I met at this point. It was something I was getting pretty good. Mapping out how the interactions were going to go, at age 10, extensively thinking about this. How are they going to react? I wasn't listening most of the time because I was comparing what I'd anticipated someone saying. Then from here, I'd start working through what would I say in response to what I thought they'd say. There are backup plans if they do or say something wrong.

This whole time, I'm focused on everything but being myself. I literally forgot to develop a "me." My personality got put on hold by me as I constructed how I wanted my life to be perceived by others. It's a lot for ten-year-old to synthesize every day. On top of this, I was not getting along with my dad, and even more, I was too scared and angry to say or do anything. I remember the day I committed to having my personality be precisely the opposite of my dad's. It's one of my stark memories. I mentally committed to altering my character, "me," to the opposite of my fathers, "me" was on hold. This had a quite an impact, a decision that's taken years to undo, but it happened. I was putting gas in the car on a family trip when I made this decision.

At home, I was getting better at lying to suit the situation and exaggerating with groups like school and sports is just a regular thing. It was only the beginning of needing other people to make me feel good or bad about everything. I was so far from understanding my own emotions that I'd forgotten I had any. This pattern manifested into tons of shame and guilt for feeling this way.

I knew life at home was tough due to my dad's increasing volatility, and I convinced myself everyone else didn't have these things going on at their home. This wasn't accurate, most everyone did have something going on at home and with themselves. Right or not it's what I thought, and it became my story.

I'd gained more weight, and I started struggling with self-image issues more frequently, starting to change behaviors to feel a little better. This self-image issue along with anxiety about my home life began to lead me down a path of obsessing. Layer on the constant inner turmoil of being an awkward kid at this point. My experience was more complicated than it should have been, and I had little confidence to do anything about those crushes anyway back then.

Rural America to this day is impacted by an isolation effect and limited resources to address. I felt alone, there was no one I thought I could talk too. Honestly, I didn't even know people talked about issues back then. All that we saw and heard growing up back then was to suck it up and get over it.

"Knowing your own darkness is the best method for
dealing with the darknesses of other people."

— CARL JUNG

First Blackout

The first time I drank to get drunk I was 14, and it was also my first blackout from drinking alcohol. It was a Junior/Senior high school after-prom party that wasn't my prom being a freshman. Pretty baller, right? Not sure that was an accurate assessment of myself, and that phrase didn't exist in the mid-'80s. I sure thought so at the time. My buddy, I'll call him Greg because it's his name, and I somehow got invited to this after-prom party. I called Greg when writing this to fact check what I remembered about it. Neither of us recalled all the details but each recalled part of this the other didn't from 30+ years ago.

It was amazing to feel part of this older crowd, invited to something that others in my peer group participated in. Even with the violent vomiting many times, I fell in love with changing how I felt using whatever I could get my hands on. This happens to be alcohol to start. No idea how we got home at 4 a.m. with no car, many miles, and several towns away from my friends' house. It was a significant coup at age 14 to participate in this shindig with an entire group of your kids. We had no business being there, but we did have a hell of a good time from what I'm able to remember.

I was drunk almost immediately, and I was flying! I felt included, amazingly for one of the first times in my whole life. Why this feeling grabbed me and made me feel so connected, I don't know, it just did. In retrospect, I was emotionally hooked and physically well on my way to getting high, incredibly high on whatever I could find, as much as I could see. It was a "high" I chased for many years. I vividly remember how excited and happy I was even at the point when I vomited outside the party again and again at 1 a.m. Momentarily it was horrible, then someone picked me up, dusted me off, and I got back to drinking. I'm a determined drinker, even the first time that I got drunk at that young age.

We were drinking beer and wine that night. Jump 25 years later I was drinking some of the world's best wine, California's finest selections toward the end of my drinking, Opus One, Caymus, and Silver Oak. So, going from a T.J. Swan blackout, it is insulting, a little nauseating, and utterly laughable in reflecting on it. I was doing the same thing with $175 a bottle wine as $3 bottle, vomiting and blacking out. It's all the same category for me as an alcoholic.

What a night. I ended up kissing an older girl that night, a girlfriend of a guy that had another side-story. When younger I thought this guy was the funniest, I wanted to be like this. Again, chasing something and someone else. His funny wasn't what I ended up aspiring to be. This whole thing seems more dramatic an evening than likely was as I write about it so many years later. Likely she felt it was cute that this little kid was shit-faced, stumbling around in a blurry partial blackout, why wouldn't you kiss him.

I'll be honest, it's a weird and awkward memory with borderline inappropriate contact at that age, in hindsight. It is a make-me-cringe moment as I write this because I'd never thought about the context. I'm not saying anything negative against the adult in the situation nor making light of the situation. This was a long time ago, I'd consider us both kids as it relates to my own experience. A 17-year-old shouldn't be kissing a 14-year-old under the influence, my point is these situations are happening every day in part because of alcohol and drug use with students. I hope these alcohol situations end and don't happen like this.

It's a prime example of how poor decisions can be made under the influence of substances, ones that would be less likely to be made sober. It was the culture at that time growing up in our community. Silly risk-taking and lots of drinking, none of us thought twice about it. The next day, I felt like death, limitless vomiting, and I couldn't wait to do it again. I'd found my version of peace—numbing myself completely.

You know, I got through this whole prom party incident without getting caught by anyone but my friends' mother. She did work our hungover little selves for the rest of the weekend. Talking about this with a friend from so many years ago was a treat, and I'm grateful for that friendship and conversation. He reminded me of lost memory.

Entirely not amusing to anyone but those who probably know Greg but I'm including it, so I don't forget this again. My friend looked in the mirror the next day while driving back from the landfill. remember his mom was punishing us with work all day, and he stated with vigor, "Mirror, mirror on the truck, I don't give a fuck." It was the first time he dropped the f-bomb in front of his mom. I'd forgotten this, thank you, Greg, for reminding me. The catching conversation made me laugh almost as hard as we did at 14 when it happened.

There were a few questions that came up later from parents and teachers but nothing more. It gave me a little reputation at that early age of being a party kid and allowed me in both our community and others to get invites for the other parties. I started obsessing full-time on how I could attend as many as possible without getting caught in my next adventure. The summer I turned fifteen I was able to find older kids to hang around with as well as summer better-paying jobs with farmers who liked to drink. Little did they know they hired the perfect driver to keep them out of trouble.

Chapter 11

Drunk Driver

MY DRIVING JOB AT AGE FIFTEEN encompassed illegally picking up booze-orders from the bar, which could be construed by some as somewhat complicated for a 15-year-old. Well no, it wasn't in central Nebraska in the '80s. It consisted of going to the bar, ordering correctly, getting the order (one-two cases of beer and six-pack of orange soda).

Yes, as God is my witness, I would walk in with cash or not (they worked off credit) with the ordering system. Then I'd receive the common question: Is this really for "insert name" I was working for at that time, my answer "yep," then walk out with the delivery. It was a different time and place, that is for sure. Illegally driving, acquiring and possessing alcohol, then to cap off my crime spree, I'd drink beer on the way back and blame the bar owner for shorting me. My bosses never questioned and likely never believed me either.

In rural America, in the early '80s, it was simpler and much less expensive to have your 15-year-old driver get caught without a license and fix the problem than getting arrested for driving while intoxicated again for a 2nd to 10th time. If you had several previous arrests for DWI, this was fraught with illegal bits but better than killing someone else or yourself on dangerous gravel roads.

I got my official first driving and alcohol buying job before having a license or being able to pay taxes. Those days of participating in straight-forward victimless (or least I thought so) crimes should be long gone, and retrospectively I'd categorize this as a corruption of my youth. No judgment on the people I worked for as I was well on my way to be an alcoholic without them. They were secondary characters in my story. It would be ten more years before I dealt with my only driving arrest, stopped while under the influence. It was the cycle repeating itself.

The experiences likely impacted me down the road, but I don't blame anyone. I was happy about the job; I worked hard for those folks, more work than driving and buying booze, I promise you that. We worked our asses off, it was a way of life then and there. It was just another day in rural Nebraska. My apologies to the State of Nebraska for these indiscretions. I'll apologize for the other law-breaking later, I promise.

I've chosen to share a little detail about this time; you'll start to really understand how much time I dedicated to my obsession with changing my emotions by using alcohol at age fourteen. It was a pacesetter for my path to addiction and dysfunction. My freshman year in high school was a time to step up my drinking game. This resourceful 15-year-old found a buyer who supplied us—my drinking buddies and me, which I'll refer to as "the b-gang." They shall remain nameless, in case they've got any political aspirations in the future.

This is somewhat unrelated to the book and pithy at a minimum, underage drinking and drug use is more an issue that when I was 15. It was a big issue then but nothing we could have imagined it being today with children dying from overdoses daily. Society has been desensitized to problems with minor consumption of substances, it's what most consider more a "coming of age" story than "future crop of addicts" documentary. We need to work to address this, prevention is more effective and less expensive than intervention. This is if someone does die from substance use first.

The supplier, we'd negotiated a deal, a weekly drop of alcohol. "Buyer would acquire two cases of good beer, in bottles, and a pint of schnapps each week. Occasionally some other liquor such as Southern Comfort, Purple Passion or other vodkas. This was purchased from the big town not that close to Sumner, Nebraska." It helped our money go further because big city prices were better than a local bar, roughly 30% less, and the risk of getting caught was significantly lower.

I'd call this drinking economics. Anyone in recovery will so appreciate the math, we developed a supply chain for our entertainment and self-medicating. Of course, we thought about retail prices versus bulk buying at 15; we weren't Neanderthals or unintelligent about this approach. The juice on this deal was a six-pack of Budweiser bottles which was as a great deal in '80s money.

We'd pick up the weekly drop on the back porch of the buyer's place and provide the money for next week. One person would keep the booze for safe keeping in their trunk. My life centered around this weekly process for almost 3 years. It was unthinkable for many, looking back at the amount of time and money spent by children on this illegal activity. I've got to admit, it was an economically sound and a dependable fulfillment process, an entrepreneurial lot we ended up being. We basically broke the law each week, and I moved closer to a daily user of whatever, fill in the blank.

The problem was, I had no other emotional skills developed at fifteen. When the drinking started to be consistent, emotional growth stopped, and brain chemistry starts changing at this pivotal time.

Anything emotional everything halted, in many ways likely regressed a bit, such as interpersonal communication. It went on hard pause, no alcohol consumed made it harder to talk to anyone. I'd got much more outgoing with the help of alcohol frequently. Take this drug this away, I was anxious about everything. With no skills for coping with my emotions, these experiences and situations didn't allow me to find my voice, which is what many do in these developmental parts of life.

I was very focused on being someone else, who I thought others wanted me to be, I was chasing what allowed me to do this and feel better. Other than the drinking times, I have very few growing up memories that I felt great about. Not that this was accurate, but it's the truth about what I was feeling and memories I carried forward with me. There were no tools to deal with these feelings, nothing but alcohol to allow me to forget about everything until college, where I also found drugs to help with that issue.

My fall back of drinking was eating, it was short-lived and led to much worse feelings of emptiness and isolation, then drinking more to try and find that place. It was harder to see that sweet spot of not caring but being in some control. The cycle I was in was unhealthy, but I was an excellent addict. Ready to take everything to the extreme. I was able to present an outward life that was positive, funny, and functional, basically what I wanted life to be. It was not what it was though. The medicating was my primary coping skill from 14 until 40-years-old. These set patterns of problematic and higher risk behaviors.

You might be saying to yourself, what was wrong with the kid? I was an addict, holding it together with grades, sports, some friends, and work. Most of my activities were not supportive of healthy relationships. Who knew my little drinking experiences in my teens would engulf my life for the next 27 years? The reality is my life has changed forever in part from this.

Chapter 12

Fat Feelings

I STARTED TO GAIN MORE WEIGHT, and coaches liked this because I was more significant physically than a typical 15-year-old at that time. My typical peer was 120 pounds and gangly. I was big enough, about 180, determined, and just mean deep enough inside me to excel at contact sports like football. There was a contrast between weighing more being good for playing games and what was right for my self-image. I felt fat, self-conscious, and not like everyone else my age. My inner narrative was very negative, almost all the time. The negative thoughts stopped when I drank—no drugs in high school oddly enough, and I'm grateful for this not starting until college.

Ironically, I felt those druggy kids were out of control back then. Funny thing, I'd just not had an opportunity to try drugs in high school or who knows what I would have done. I was busy being out of control with alcohol.

Lots of beer on the weekend but drinking beer during school was considerably harder after I turned 16; it required a different strategy. I started drinking during the day at school. It was a small school, everyone knew everyone. Drinking beer was somewhat noticeable in a group of kids at school who smelled of either sweat or bubble gum. I needed to move to clear liquor, total alcoholic in the making here in hindsight. What was happening was an unlocking of a consistent pattern of drinking each day for me. That's when Purple P. hit the scene in the '80s; it was

70

grape malt liquor. It did the trick, and it was harder to catch me at school.

I was getting more hammered and blacking out, coming home late, and dangerously racing cars blurry as I was turning 16. My parents had no idea because I was good at hiding these activities from them, a fantastic liar from lots of practice.

When I hear issues happen with kids about this age or younger, I don't think twice about it because they're likely just as good or better than me of hiding it from the parents while not getting in trouble and pulling good grades. It's possible, I was doing 35 years ago.

Age Sixteen

I had wrecked three cars by the time I was 18 years old. As a functioning alcoholic, I was good at making up stories and delivering the tales to my mom and dad in addition to anyone else I needed. I've forgotten more than I can begin to apologize for but again, I'm sorry about all the messes.

I was a pretty good storyteller, and I was able to keep my account straight, most of the time anyway. My dad was wild as a kid, and I'm reasonably sure he didn't believe I was as sketchy and as out of control as him because I didn't get into fights, my behavior didn't result in a battered outside. I was getting my ass kicked on the inside. I was just a different type of risk-taker but positively as deviant or maybe worse. Only somehow, I didn't have a lot of consequences. Part of this was living in a small town and getting caught by the sheriff that my dad used to help when needed. Sherriff didn't want me to get into trouble; he knew my dad would lose it with me if I got arrested, so he'd take the alcohol. I was a generally well-liked and kind person to people in general, he didn't want me in that much trouble. This seems standard thought process, especially in a small town back then.

As I shared earlier, I'd committed to being nothing like my father based on our relationship while I was growing up. I was becoming more like him than I'd ever thought, and I am still like him today. I'm able to see lots of good things these days though.

Chapter 13

Find the Party

I WAS COMING INTO MY OWN with finding parties, a superpower of mine at 16-years-old. Had the cash from working a lot, and a vehicle I'd not wrecked yet which increased my range to see all my drinking friends and party as much as I possibly could. It's not clear to me why or how I started to go to other towns for parties. My friends didn't drink enough, or they had girlfriends or jobs, something I suppose was the catalyst for me expanding my drinking circle. It didn't take me long to find friends from the most prominent party school in our area; it was 40 miles away. They liked to drink just like me, a lot and often.

This group of kids had money and less resistance to partying. They took more risks and had parents who didn't get in the way of all the fun they and I wanted to have. It started a 27-year driving while drunk or high career that I'm genuinely grateful daily, and thank God, probably not thanking often enough; I never killed anyone while driving under the influence.

Today, knowing how I operated, one of my biggest concerns about being out later in the evening is getting hit by someone like me, back when I was drinking and driving. I've had a couple of friends, in active recovery, A.A. friends who were killed by drunk drivers. I'm sure wherever they ended up in the afterlife, they irony on them is not lost. It sure wouldn't be on me.

I didn't remember driving 40 miles home many times over two years.

It's terrifying to think much about how often I don't remember the trip. I only wrecked one of the three cars I've crashed while making these trips around rural Nebraska to party, another miracle in my book.

My drinking was progressing quickly, that's how it worked, addiction especially alcoholism is a progressive disease. You never regress, you stop then start right as bad as you left it. As you progress into the physical dependency, more is needed to be useful, effective keeps moving farther away until no amount will do the trick any longer. You physically start rejecting the alcohol, because your body won't process enough to get you the place that you had known in the past. A calm, more peaceful place that you're numb from the emotions. It was spiraling faster than manageable any longer I would have been in serious trouble then a break came when I was able to graduate mid-senior year at 17-years-old. I'd enlisted into the Army National Guard. The Army basic and advanced training in Ft. Knox Kentucky started on January 4, 1987. I remember that day very clearly; I was terrified, a scared 17-year-old that had never been off the farm without family more than a few hours.

I'd do anything to get away from my life and start a new one. This meant even leaving all that I knew, be willing to stop drinking every day because I'd pay for college which gave me more independence to get wasted all the time. My thought process wasn't that clear or intentional as I'd spelled out, I just wanted to be done with high school and move on. It was a good idea to enlist. I have no regrets and am proud to have served my state and country with the Army. The performance in the national guard wasn't always high due to my using escalating significantly in part with those I was in the guard duty. When I got to university, into a fraternity, and had full independence, I basically immersed into addiction.

The Army National Guard was the answer to everything in my small world. It was my first geographic move in active addiction. For those not familiar with recovery terms, a "geographic" is when moving is an addict's solution. It never worked because I can't move away from myself, I tried this several times.

Yes, I went to the army, training lasted for five months. There was no drinking for two and a half months until the halfway point weekend in my time in Kentucky. We got two days off away from the army post (base). I found a group who wanted to party in my training company. I got entirely wasted, blackout drunk, and that's kind of all I remember from my training weekend. It was one of a hundred blackouts over 27 years of drinking and using. I didn't drink for two months more, and when I got back it was a boom, dropped right back into the life I wanted to escape so desperately. My daily drinking kicked off shortly after I returned and as I've learned happened, progressed from where I left it, then quickly got worse.

Chapter 14

Finally, Graduation

A BRIEF THANK-YOU NOTE TO MY high school classmates: you were unbelievably thoughtful to me back then. I probably half-heartily said thanks. My classmates scheduled our senior prom after I returned from training. It's touching to remember that, chokes me up a bit to this day that anyone really cared, at least that is the way I remember it. Whatever happened, it's a sweet memory. Thank you.

I was close to 18-years-old, and I'd already been to basic training and graduated from high school. Found a job with my drinking buddies, working for their family who I always figured would take me all those years that I was struggling at home, just in case when things blew up at home. It never happened, but I still think they would have done that, thank you. They had what appeared to be more normal home life, the dad and granddad both called me by my last name. Mom and grandma of friends were entirely kind to me. I felt like I belonged back then.

It was tenser at home with my taste of and pushed for more independence under my parents' roof. Drinking more and more everything felt like a fight with my dad, likely because I couldn't stay drunk 24/7 as much as I would have liked it too and did try. With my job, I was with my friends a lot more, basically all the time, so we drank a lot. It started to be every day, all day, drinking when I was 17. Then I went to college, and the drinking got considerably worse, epically worse within weeks.

Off to my alcohol nirvana, that summer, still only 17, I went to meet a freshman roommate assigned randomly for the dorms. Oh, did we hit it off? I got wasted, vomited several times within five hours of meeting him, and he was cool with it. Then a few weeks later, a rush weekend at the only college I applied, guess what? I got blackout drunk and felt like the life of the party. It was a school known for being a party school. I'd partied there with friends when I was in high school. Might have been the same ones who invited me to the after-prom party at age 14. This was the place for me, I could get lost in the bigger crowd while losing myself at the same time, and it seemed reasonable.

It was a good sign for fun and free times ahead. I couldn't wait to go to college, get blackout wasted, meet people. This whole thing clicked about drinking and being free. The way I like to drink wasn't a problem at university; it was an idyllic culture suited for me, as an active alcoholic and aspiring drug addict. University didn't let me down; it almost killed me.

I was on the steep slope of opening a whole other type of issue; it just flooded like someone swung open a floodgate, once I could rage with any substance, freely as I'd wanted to do. That was the beginning of complete submersion into alcohol; drugs and just about anything that make the world faster and number. It was vast and with limited consequences for a year. Then entirely a surprise to me at age 19, it started to fall apart quickly. I was drunk and high for the next five years, pretty much every single day. I almost died from a cocaine overdose while playing basket-ball, so I started to try and stop getting high, within 3 years I was done with drugs. Then only got more drunk from the strongest alcohol I could find right up until the day I stopped. I am not sure if I found recovery or recovery found me.

Sober Is Better: Part Two

W E'VE ARRIVED, IT'S THE SECOND PART of the book; it's my bitesize thoughts and stories. My short shares are designed to stand on their own; you won't miss out on anything by picking up the book and opening to a single story. Some gracious people have shared they keep my first book by their nightstand and randomly open to a story.

There are some of my stories and references that might resonate and make more sense to those in recovery but keep reading. All of these are various life lessons I've learned through healing with some through a lens of addiction, others through active recovery from emotional traumas. The messages, learnings, and lifestyle apply to everyone, either someone you care about or yourself.

I've done my best to share in a way that might make sense for everyone. Again, thank you, I'm honored you started the book, and extra psyched you've made it this far. Trigger alert, I talk about abuse, various trauma, and suicide in this section.

Chapter 15

Summer of Love

I'M A LEO, BORN IN CALIFORNIA in the summer of 1969. My birth is synonymous with "love, sex, drugs, and rock-n-roll" with Woodstock but also think Neil Armstrong and the Vietnam War. It feels looking back at that period as though 1969 was a year filled with contrast, extremes, and chaos, interspersed with culture shifts, changing ideologies, and people finding then sharing their voices.

We have an opportunity to participate in the coming years in another significant shift in priorities with ideologies and kindness as a society. It could very well be much the same as in 1969 change. Please read and share my short thoughts and experiences with anyone that might need it, I'm hopeful and thankful it will be the genesis of many conversations.

Learning to Feel

A few years into the recovery from alcoholism, I progressed into stage three of my recovery from alcohol addiction. I've categorized recovery into stages that align with various levels of activities, maintenance, and learning in my recovery process. For me, stage-zero is the first 12 months, stage-one is 12 months to five years, stage-two from five to ten years, stage-three ten to 15 years, stage-four 15 to 25 years. I'll figure out the next stage when I get there.

I'm now in recovery at a stage referred to as long-term recovery

(LTR) stage-three. This means I'm not that new to not drinking, and I've learned many of the coping skills required to live a productive and full life. There are a few areas that I'm continuing to work even after ten years in recovery.

One of the best parts of accumulating a few days in a row of sobriety is I know a few more things than when I first got sober. I've heard tons of great things related to getting sober, relapsing and dying from this brutal but manageable disorder. The most important things for me about being aware of oneself in recovery is an ability to ask for help and share your story with others in recovery. Those who might be struggling to get sober, find a community that understand recovery. If we do this alone, it will likely kill us and maybe others. Together as a community, we're not alone, ever again and everyone is better for asking for help.

Recently, I woke up one morning feeling horrible because of inane yet uncomfortable sinus trouble. Horrible these days is so much better than my first day of sobriety. Lousy back then was despair and hopelessness, being lost within myself and battling a void in every sense of the word doesn't come with an obvious path to feeling better. Today, I just feel a little off because of ordinary things, not from drinking into an unconsciousness.

In recovery, I've learned what healing means, what trauma looks like, and how we've all experienced different challenges in our lifetimes. I've heard thousands of people share, met them as they're trying to recover from whatever has taken over their life. Peace is available, but it's not available without treating the pain, it's not easy but very possible. In recovery, we learn that our feelings are not typically the facts, they're just life experiences. We can handle these feelings; we've survived much worse before recovery.

The Real Honesty

"Be honest with me." I heard that right away in recovery at the 12-step meetings I started attending when I entered my new recovery life several years ago. The honesty message came primarily from talking to addicts and alcoholics in their journeys of recovery. I love talking with sober people; you get authentic conversations with no pretense. It's interesting that later in sobriety, years later, I'd heard another share about honesty.

> *"If you're honest with me then you're likely to be honest with 'we.'"*
>
> — UNKNOWN A.A.

So simple of a concept, yet so far removed and elusive from addicts' scrambled logic when we're actively using. When I'm not in recovery, honesty starts by admitting I want to change how I feel since my perception of life was horrible, I was never honest. My job each day is to remember each day: my life becomes horrible if I drink again.

Upon starting to get sober, you start to hear things, healthy things. You learn about tools you don't have today to process feelings less destructively in life, not just about not using alcohol, drugs, sex, and gambling. I thought to myself, "OK," and prayed to God to help me. I would do whatever it takes and learn new things to help myself. It didn't sound like much to ask me to get my life in order, to turn it into a life worth living, but it's the single most significant effort and commitment I'd ever made to myself.

This recovery process lends itself to honesty about everything in my life. As you get deeper into being sober, more time and work are likely completed which provides more feeling safe and confident with being completely honest with others but most importantly with yourself. This whole recovery thing is measured on how you treat yourself, and where you're at today with staying sober as a lifestyle. Those are two main focuses, especially in the early days of being sober. The healing requires an equivalent time as the trauma controlled your life. Doing your best with honesty when you begin early sobriety, learning to ask yourself more intentional questions is an essential building block in the new stage of your life.

It will happen; it's easy for the questions to come, but the answers are hard—don't let this give you an excuse to drink. It's not worth it; it will never be better if you use it again. Maybe there will be false relief for a few minutes, but then you're spiraling back into a living hell. It is where you ask for help. Pretty much every step of the way, you ask for help. I'll be the first to admit it made me uncomfortable but learning to pray, and ask for help, saved my life, and probably will save yours as well. Praying doesn't mean to a Christian god, it can be to any higher power, buddha, or god of your understanding.

Just like being sober, this being honest with yourself takes practice. Practice honesty, candid honesty with questions like "Do I want help?" and "Did you drink today?" It's a long miraculous journey that we're on together; this is where it starts, not ends. Let's get to practice these small things. If I can do it, anyone can find sobriety and happiness.

Chapter 16

Thoughts Lost

AWARENESS AND DAYDREAMING SEEM TO BE a gift as I get a little bit older and end up spending an excessive amount of time feeling sorry about things I didn't get done today. My mind with the help of tons of experiences and stimuli overloads each day tends to wish to focus on multiple items at one time. It doesn't really work, I just feel it works at times. With intention and meditation, I've gotten better at prioritizing my thoughts which impacts my day.

The tools learned in sobriety, and recovery lifestyle provides a good keystone for prioritizing and expanding my level of awareness I'm currently in a while writing this book.

By the time I completed this previous paragraph, it had reminded me of the need for a simple approach to my sobriety and recovery life which I share below; it's my 10 steps in my daily action plan:

- sober first with each action
- be willing more than not
- don't use
- ask for help
- give help
- do the work
- be kind to yourself
- stretch your legs

- exercise your mind
- be grateful

My Gods

I have rejected, questioned, and embraced gods of many types over the years. In recovery, I've adopted a 12 step-support program, A.A. to be specific, in addition to therapy, and meditation. I'll pretty much do anything I need to when it comes to staying sober. I've waxed and waned on what my and everyone's version of God looks like to me. It occupied quite a lot of my time and energy for a couple of years until recently. I concluded that I'm too literal in my segmentation of what the many versions of spirituality look like today. My best answer is a well-rounded spiritual program, embracing and believing what's needed to be sober.

Those in recovery openly challenge the organized religion version of a Christian God; there are many reasons for questioning and challenging. We're a very literal bunch in recovery when it suits of course. I start healing spiritually; then my God evolves into more than a construct for debate. Humanity all need a god in some form, some days, for some reason. That form of God is hope, faith, or maybe loving something, something better than us today.

Then one day, I was in a meeting, someone shared how they discovered and embraced a god of their understanding, it was when they gave up thinking about God as a religion. I've been resistant to organized religions, at times overtly rejected them. It's my sense of what appears to be a rigid doctrine, this is what I've continued to struggle with until I didn't care any longer and focused on my own made-local spiritual program.

I see fellow alcoholics in pain, needing to believe in anything—whether it's a god or not—to survive. They're holding on to life by a thin line. As they struggle into sobriety, they continue to move forward and heal because of hope then faith in something, it's beautiful to see in action. Someone shared this with us one time, actually many people several times: "Make whatever you need your god, and just find something spiritual to work with you to stay sober."

"Whatever" could be a meeting, a workout at the gym, a meditation prayer or mantra. There are many options for what your god could be. If you wanted to ask if I feel we need something spiritual to connect with in recovery to heal, the answer is yes, I do believe something is necessary. What that concept might be isn't for me to say. It was for me, at the very least, connection with other addicts that kept me sober. I could see hope and faith working, day by day in people's lives. That was my god for a while. I'm sober so far, so it's working for me.

My way can't be the only way to find recovery and sobriety, but it's sure one way to try. I readily admit recovery could be within yourself, a type of self-spirit that you tap into for healing, guidance, and growth. My opinions are shared to help offer my experience, not any dogma or belief system as a gospel; this is for sure. Please try to find your way to recovery, ask for help, and try one or 100 times in whatever way possible, keep trying until it works.

Chapter 17

Kindness is Courage

IT STARTED WITH A WHOLE BUNCH of conflicting actions toward others and me. Such as being kind to others, chasing acceptance, self-worth, no place, purpose, and kindness for myself. I could give help and provide support but couldn't take either, much less ask for help. Indeed, I couldn't accept help and kindness; it was foreign, uncomfortable, and unwanted. I didn't feel I warranted any of these positive things. Before I got sober, this is how I lived and thought every single minute, it was complete chaos.

I wasn't capable of being honest with myself, much less anyone else. One of the gifts I've received in recovery is an awareness of when I'm not kind and honest to others. As important is when I'm not empathetic, and fair to myself. This never happened when I was actively using. I had to learn the difference between feeling empathetic and self-pity. These elements are what make up my concept of "kindness is courage."

It has involved a lot of personal work, years of working through what clouded my life and connection with others. A simple kindness to myself for what needs to get done each day starts to show up when I'm working on my recovery. If I'm not delivering self-care and working on "self," I won't be effective or efficient in helping others.

It all converges together, continuing to be courageous, I've got to help myself be healthy and present first, or none of what I'm doing is sustainable. It becomes so short-lived and fleeting. My sharing with others how to heal and find a recovery lifestyle is a large part of the work. Unless I am on the same journey, as I'm sharing about it feels limiting when talking to others about recovery. I've seen my healing grow, and emotional growth progress from a place of pain, transforming into kindness and love.

Addicts in recovery know what this looks like; we recognize our own straight away. I can pick "us" out of a crowd. It's that vibe of being aware and thankful, filled with gratitude based on what life used to be like and what it's like now. Everyone who's human possesses free-will which comes with the pain of some kind; we just can't help it. It's incredible when growth, healing, and recovery happens, and you shed some of the long-standing pain. When I see or even hear about this, it makes me remember it's always possible, and I'll never be alone again.

Willingness NOW Foundation

My wife Michella and I started a charity named the Willingness NOW Foundation. The mission of WNF is improving the lives of people impacted by addiction and mental health challenges. WNF is working on three programs:

- Assessment Innovation — Improving clinical addiction assessments used to enhance treatment efficacy by developing mental health and addiction recovery treatment science.
- Mental Health First Aid training — Certifying as many people from veteran's organizations, first responders, healthcare, and human resources.
- Outreach — Connecting with those who feel they don't belong, are alone, and struggle with hope.

My life today is made up of a recovery lifestyle and philosophy; this has taught me to embrace universal spirituality, open-mindedness, and therapies as keystones to recover from addiction. To keep my sobriety, it's my responsibility to offer support and give back to those still suffering. There are many ways I believe an individual will get and stay sober; willingness must be the first step for it to work. My hope is all that try will find their way.

The Questions

The HALT (hungry, angry, lonely, tired) acronym is used quite often when referencing tools dealing with the concepts of self-care, recovery, and emotional management. I hear it referenced with anxiety and wellness in general. It's nice to have my worlds start to converge.

It's surprising when checking out the situation, how you feel, or your actions against the question, "Are you hungry, angry, lonely or tired?" This root cause analysis of why you lost it or felt unusually upset could open your eyes. Try it next time, like tomorrow.

HALT

- Hungry
- Angry
- Lonely
- Tired

HALT applies to me 80% of the time. There is a spectrum, and it affects at varying levels. I feel the lack of sleep is the big one to watch for me. Research supports that 71% of adults are lacking sleep regularly. What I want to believe why this gets talked about so much, is because it's true, it works. When I'm hungry, I make poor and unhealthy decisions about food and life. If I've allowed myself to get angry, I'm reacting to feelings that are snap-judgment-type emotions versus well thought out responses. When lonely, there have been many deviations, such as fear of rejection, self-consciousness, my feelings getting hurt, and many more.

And being tired, a lack of sleep has a very similar effect to alcohol and drugs on your brain. Responsiveness, cognitive impairment, snap judgments—all of these are available with lack of sleep. There are so many examples of how research supports this simple and impactful tool called HALT.

Chapter 18

Feed Your Brain

WHAT FEEDS MY BRAIN, HEART, AND soul? It depends, all of these are always my answer. I crave and require different content, meditation, podcasts, audiobooks, paperbacks, articles, and digital scripture. I've finally given up in searching for an outcome, content that checks all my boxes, all or nothing. This box of material doesn't exist. I've put in a box that will fulfill and inspire me.

Now, I search based on what I'm doing, what I'm feeling, and what gets put in front of me. This organic filling of the trough has been resulting in more consumption of content and information. It also felt better. It's a little harder because I use less control to select, and more feelings to direct me to what I need to hear, read, and see. I've practiced telling myself it's not a waste of time. It helped open me to exploring silly, intense, and sexy types of content.

Adoption

What we think, why we emote a certain way, emotions and feelings are a critical part of us. A topic like understanding feelings as a concept is harder to get your head around if you're early in addiction recovery. It was hard because I was emotionally raw, and physically a little fuzzy still. As addicts, we've spent a lifetime trying not to feel anything any longer. What was going on with our emotions was not something we worried about when actively using. Burying the fear, pain, and feelings of being nothing was the priority. These are all genuine feelings that were always in the background of my life. I was a good actor in my play, my story, most wouldn't have guessed how lousy life felt, what the void was all about with me.

I'm not unique; it's prevalent to hear someone in recovery wondering about trying sobriety like test-driving a car you'd like to purchase. It doesn't work that way, something that took many years to get to recovery doesn't get fixed quickly or on your timeline. Be patient, do the work, it's a game of inches that add up to miles with time.

Not a Dream

Addicts don't wake up as children with a goal of injecting heroin, to survive the day, or blacking out from a bottle of gin. It's accumulated pain with limited knowledge, support, and awareness of what to do. Learning how to work on and treat trauma and emotional extremes driving substance misuse, dependency, and harmful behaviors are getting into layers of recovery.

Feeling something other than hating yourself could take a little while. It's likely a new feeling. My survival tools formed early in life, some would say because I had an early trauma. I don't know what started it, but I know my misery ended it. I've made progress on what elements impact my behaviors. I'm not sure of the start of the middle yet; it's something I've been digging into a few years into recovery. It's about unpacking more of my bags, starting to delve into the unconscious, an excellent example of why I am enlisting the use of professional therapy to assist in this work.

Survived

I walk into the world each day with gratitude; I'm utterly thankful I'm not dead or in prison for accidentally taking someone else's life while driving under the influence. It could have happened 50 times. It didn't by the grace of my version of God.

What being in recovery and around people in recovery allows me is practicing empathy and experiencing authentic conversations about horrible trauma individuals have endured and survived to rebuild their lives, heal the wounds of the past. Real pain inflicted on an addict by someone other than themselves—this trauma started the cycle, the cycle of chasing an escape from the pain.

We don't know how to feel better, so we learn how not to feel at all. It's survival and an empty existence of which I'm glad I went through it and found recovery. It provides me a basis to understand levels of suffering as a sufferer, healing as the healed. I wouldn't wish it on or not for anyone else, that's not my wish to convey. People are resilient beyond my comprehension, we survive and learn to turn a page in a book, we couldn't see before recovery with healing, and build a life worth living.

Chapter 19

Acting

CHANGE AND CHALLENGES ARE ALL AROUND me, opportunity and risk everywhere around me. As I move further from active addiction to long-term recovery, I learn to recognize these opportunities and chances and then do something about them.

What you hear early in recovery:

> *"This is a program of action; it's the doing not the wanting or needing."*
>
> — UNKNOWN

As you get some time sober and the fog clears, you start to get help with trauma, mental and physical health recovery and life become different. Yes, I'm doing and still do the work necessary; it's hard but better than dying. I like what I see in sobriety versus being wasted and miserable. The difference is two things:

a) My willingness to change, stopping unhealthy actions and starting healthy habits.

b) I've learned to ask for help; I admit I can't find recovery alone.

If I ever stop being willing to do the work in recovery, my chances of relapse increase significantly. I might not slip today, next week or next year but I'll be on what the old-timers call a dry-drunk which is horrible torture of the worst kind, it's a slow emotional and spiritual death.

They're miserable; you're not sober when you're on an emotional relapse. Acting means doing the work, every single day, maybe not every minute but a day.

> *"Change how you think, then your actions will change."*
> — BILL R.

Real Safety

In early sobriety, everything feels so damn raw and touchy. I remember every comment grading against me, I tried to never take all my thoughts as being very personal back to me. I settled on an emotional sunburn, anything that touched me just made me cringe. I kept working on my recovery, going to meetings, talking with other alcoholics and addicts when suddenly, not so suddenly, my life got better. It didn't feel as raw; some things started to make more sense. It's important to find those safe places whether it's a support meeting, a therapist's office, your bedroom with the door closed, a treadmill with ear-buds in, or whatever safe place you can find to begin that the healing process.

Surrender

Self-centeredness is powerful; addiction is entirely about self + trauma + survival of how lousy life makes you feel. We evolve from feeling anxious and unsettled into survival mode. I know I'm wired with DNA to survive even the worst things if necessary. Surviving and living are very different things, and an alcoholic, I'd confused them for a long time, this is part of living wounded. To manage all this, it requires a level of distorting the bad feelings and escaping from pain until you find enlightenment or misery to surrender to asking someone for help. An addict's mind works in a way that three is always better than one, and it can never work fast enough.

More is still better, it's something we all watch out for in recovery. It's who we are. If the solution takes away the pain, then my addiction tells me that's a softer and more comfortable way then dealing with the cause of the pain.

The more I want this fix versus figure out whatever issues are going on, again addiction oversees this thinking. Taking it away quickly and entirely, even when hurtful to myself, is the absolute brutality of addiction. It's a cruel cycle; it does just the opposite long-term—the using drives a person to use more and gives you less. The moving line of escape in your head exacerbated the feeling of emptiness and hopelessness when my addiction promised me peace by applying and then a reality that peace is never attainable this way.

It's what was at the bottom; it was recovery or death. Those felt like my only options, and indeed there was only one—recovery and I grabbed ahold of it for dear life.

Myself

It's years into my recovery, and I am considerably more confident in what my inner narrative runs about continually. I'm less fearful and more exploratory with this inner voice. I use it in the outside world with all of you, but on the inside, it still waxes and wanes on what to do and when to do it. Why a person does and says things, we always have a reason, even if we can't admit or acknowledge it. I'm just acting very human as a person in recovery.

I have embraced not feeling wrong about that lack of confidence on occasion, but instead of handling the situation reactively, I dig into finding a solution. It's alright to admit I don't know what to do. The solutions consist of going deeper into the why of what's going on. It's part of learning tools to manage emotions and adequately respond with information I've gained in listening to my recovery process.

Addict Talk

Am I too sensitive and am I overreacting? These were my thoughts before recovery; they looped in my head. I worked on that; there are so many times my initial thoughts before my recovery were all about me. This still happens but know, it's not my feeling of brokenness and lack of worthiness. A solution can be as simple as giving myself permission to feel my emotions, sensing something is always alright. Now, it's let me figure out a solution to make me calm, whatever's going on with you is yours, not mine. That is the inner dialogue that my recovery-self is processing.

Every alcoholic out there feeling like they're carrying around 1000 pounds on their chest from their entire life of coming up short, continual nothing. It's our disease telling there are a 1000 pounds—it's not there. The same voice could be telling us, I'm got this because I'm carrying all this weight distributed across all the people in recovery, 1 pound per person is entirely possible to lift the total weight and more when it comes your way.

I don't know all the answers, no one does. It's because we are always learning, changing, doing resets and recovers. It's called being human as evolve with more experiences. This is the message I wish I could personally tell everyone who was entering recovery—We all had to start, had learned this stuff. But not everyone gets started, so they don't ever make it.

In recovery, I must learn the skills to figure out a way to process all those sick and good feelings, fear and confidence, love and hate, and the rest of what makes up how we think and feel in our lives. It's a lot better life when I can turn these into healthier, more forgiving, kinder to myself thoughts and behavior.

Chapter 20

Progress

"PROGRESS NOT PERFECTION" IS ONE OF the trite sayings used in the recovery community that either annoys or assures you that all will be alright; this whole recovering thing takes some time. Well, the longer you're sober, the more real these sayings become, as you fix and fit all the glaring issues into a solution early and often. Getting better in sobriety turns out to be your lifestyle. Then layer two starts with uncovering more complex and unexplained emotional bruises and scars; progress transforms into part of the daily reflection. Just making a little bit of progress on being impatient or judgmental is a big deal, this wiring is deep and real in yourself.

Most give up quickly on the perfection idea but giving up and not stewing over it is drastically different. All addicts and alcoholics stew over many things, little, big, new, old; it doesn't matter, we do. The goal is making a little progress here and there, talking about the stumbles, talking about when you get your balance back. It's all part of your story, share it in whatever way you feel makes sense to help your recovery.

Be Right

"Be right or be happy." I heard Cindy D. on a podcast share about her new sober tips for those rolling into recovery early recovery. It's good advice for any with one day or ten thousand days of sobriety.

Let's break this down: "Be right." Well, alcoholics are legendary for our ability to rationalize our superiority with any topic, with all the vim and vigor of a Marine taking the next hill. Part of what we work through is slowing down the I'm right-your wrong pattern long enough to get sober, then learn some self-awareness so that being right has absolutely no value to our recovery, zero. It just doesn't matter.

"Be happy." Is this a fleeting emotion, a behavior, a foundational personality trait? And what is happy? Well, light morphs from calm, too relaxed, then satisfied, to well-rested. For me, happiness is being satisfied with actions, thoughts, and feelings all going back to the basics. I'm going to reconstruct the phrase: "Be right or live happily." This helps my simple mind remember it. We learn it doesn't matter, be calm, and get some sleep. When you wake up if something is still bothering you, ask for help. You need it. This likely feels like an odd stream of thought, but that's pretty much this whole book, in a paragraph. It's how I've learned to think, and how I like a life I enjoy today. Be happy friends!

Chapter 21

A.A. Diversity

I WAS RECENTLY DOING RESEARCH FOR the future book when I came across the demographic breakdown for the A.A. population. I was a little surprised that 88% of the A.A. population was white. My immediate question is what the reason for the lack of diversity in the program is? If a group is attracted at some point why don't they stay? This concerns me because for some reason people of color are not drawn to a support program that could get them sober and save their life. It means something isn't working and needs to be fixed.

COMPOSITION OF A.A. MEMBERSHIP
- Men 62%
- Women 38%
- White 89%
- Hispanic 3%
- Black 4%
- Native American 1%
- Asian 1%
- Other 2%

Data from ALCOHOLICS ANONYMOUS 2014 MEMBERSHIP SURVEY

Does the philosophy of attraction versus recruitment of alcoholics only exacerbate the lack of diversity? Not a lot of answers on this question. I did see approved literature translated in Spanish, and a website is available in English, French, and Spanish with other information that was for ethnicity-specific groups.

It's an area of opportunity for Alcoholics Anonymous to evolve, so even more, people find and stay in recovery. We need innovation and evolution just as much in the treatment of substance use disorders as we need in other sectors of healthcare and industry.

I've read several articles, mostly opinion-based by those in recovery, and those who attend or have attended A.A. meetings. I bring this up not with solutions only to highlight awareness, not to be complicit in the problem. A.A. is the most established and adopted support group recovery program in the world. The lack of diversity question is one I'm going to continue to research as I work another book that might end up about diversity in recovery.

As part of the recovery community, we have work on improving advocacy and accessibility for the minority communities. Equal access to recovery must be figured out, it should be a given, but it's not. The disease of addiction is an entirely equal opportunity, recovery access, and attraction needs to mirror this equality. A.A. must figure this out. Meetings are available around the world in so many different cities and locations, but it's not working. 88% white isn't recovery diversity, and we're losing people of color, culture, and gender to the disease or because of this issue. I'm starting to think about it and hope more will join me in finding solutions to this issue.

Chapter 22

It Shifts

SHIFTING AN ENTIRE PERSPECTIVE IS POSSIBLE. I get frustrated, sometimes justifiably but mostly because whatever it is didn't go the way I
expected. Yes, it sounds very human to feel these emotions. It could be I
didn't anticipate any surprises, and sudden twists and turns are coming
at me. The question then for me becomes, why does change bother me
and how can I adapt to limit change bothering me.

It has been suggested to me, it's like looking at a tree, and you can't
see around the tree. You can't see through the tree, but if you learn a little
right or left, you can now see around it with no problem. This now needs
to become my thought process, shift things slightly, help myself let go of
frustration. It's not quite that easy to change things, but with practice,
it works well eventually being very natural. At times I've got to ask for
help, talk it through with someone to gain objectivity. By this time, with
all the effort to understand my issue, I've got the "why," and the shift has
revealed itself.

Shame

As I learn about what creates and eliminates shame, I understand
what shame entails. I have started breaking down what shame means to
me. I didn't really understand how profound and involved the impact has
been on my journey in recovery and life. My conscious self in recovery is

enlisting professional help, some therapy to unlock the unconscious part of what I'm still carrying around and why I've held on to these feelings for so many years.

I know when something is bothering me, and I just can't put my finger on it. That box, sealing up on a shelf is right there, it's got a weight to it. What I've learned in recovery after several years was how to unpack the bigger less obvious emotional bags. I'm staying tuned for what is to come, it's a fluid process, it happens as soon as I'm ready.

Shame is one of the most dangerous emotions. It's complicated and a self-conscious feeling along with guilt, and pride. I end up having these negative loops playing in my head that just pop-up, with no warning. The loop could be triggered by a comment, look, opinion, and action. It all brings up what I feel worst about in myself. These feelings I map back to shame and fear, this is also where I resolve these issues with positive thoughts, and a process to work through the thought loop.

> "You were sick, but now you're well again, and there's work to do."
>
> — Kurt Vonnegut, Timequake

More Money

Seven years into my active yet still functional alcoholism. In my late 20s, I was doing well financially, considerably above average, although I was a physical and emotional wreck. My job was managing an $80 million business for a larger company. It was quite challenging, the most significant number of people I'd been responsible for managing. The company had moved me around the U.S., Puerto Rico, and the U.K., working for the various divisions. The money and job got bigger, quickly—stock options, revenue responsibility, and more people to manage. I did well at the role. Finally, toward the end, I was promoted to a board position with the company who by this time was publicly traded. My last job where I was over $300 million in sales, 1200 people in my group. This was a low-point in depression, despair, and self-destruction. This the first time I've mentioned depression, it the first time I can guess I was overcome by it.

The working culture was horribly toxic, which I fit right into, it was my inside matching the outside. The toxicity was likely what enabled me to be successful, I spoke the language. 24-years-old and nothing but work as my priority. I was a horrible husband and step-father at this stage in my life, active alcoholism was getting worse quickly. We worked 90 hours per week, many of the weeks. I'm describing so many situations that current addicts and not are embroiled with no way out but drink or use.

This period in my mid-twenties is when I received my one arrest for DWI. I navigated the system, ending up with yet again limited consequences. I never lost my license, never had to stop driving, never missed work, and ultimately it was never on my driving or criminal record with a lot of money and plea deal. The worst part back then was it made it bumpy at home for a while, but with time, all was forgotten.

Despite leading the company in performance, the day came; the CEO fired me due to my alignment with another executive who was terminated, he didn't like me, and he was an asshole. I'm thankful he decided it was my time to go; I wasn't prepared to leave the company on my own. I share this situation because no one cared with the leadership, everyone was drinking and participating in activities that never should have been tolerated. You hit your sales and profit numbers, it was all fine.

Back then it was an overtly misogynistic organization, which wasn't my thing, thank goodness. I was fair, and everyone got a chance if you worked hard and was honest. I'm able to thank my parents for showing me this innate fairness no matter of gender, culture, and ethnicity. This toxic work environment, many gave way to the pressures but even deep into my addiction; this part of my integrity stayed intact.

In reflecting, I was aggressive and talented, inexperienced with some moral challenges which were fueled by my battle with alcohol addiction. It was a culture of hiring young, work/play hard types, with some minimum computer skills and a propensity for risk-taking. I grew-up in daily risk-taking with a family farm, this seemed reasonable.

Toxic Culture

Company culture encouraged working 80 hours a week, no work/life balance was encouraged or tolerated. Management would openly refer to you as "gay" or worse if you wanted time off. Even as an active alcoholic, I wasn't an asshole, so those were never my words. Such a toxic and unhealthy culture to work in, most stayed for the money. Admittedly, 25 years later, I admit I was complicit in not educating and stopping those who created a hostile workplace and promoted misogynistic behaviors. I'm very sorry to those who were impacted by the directly and indirectly. Again, I never directly acted this way but could have done more to stop others.

It was a dark time with my drinking, I was completely going off the rails constantly. Money to be made everywhere if you hustled, were a risk-taker and smart with sales, I was all of these at 28. In the '90s my compensation was getting close to $250,000 with unlimited travel and partying.

I'm not proud of stumbling through a parking lot in Pompano Beach, Florida, doing a two-point plan on a hood of a Toyota Camry, vomiting whiskey consumed at the strip club with your team. I was a raging alcoholic, sick with a disease that was slowly ending my life.

It seems like I'm telling this story of someone I knew, not about me. I didn't know that person, no one did. 20+ years later with 10 years of sobriety, I can attest how different I really am.

When people in recovery share their stories, it is not about being embarrassed or proud, it's about remembering where I came from, what it was like, and where I'll end up if I go back to that lifestyle. It represents the progress I've made in recovery.

The organization I've eluded to ended up getting rid of those who were toxic few years down the road. They found the right people for the proper roles. I'm very proud of what the organization evolved into today. They provide job opportunities to more than a million people a year.

Chapter 23

Work

THE HARDEST AND BEST LESSONS ABOUT self-awareness in recovery have come out of work, putting in time doing a job for money. Communicating with clients, colleagues, and management are like being in a relationship. It's 1/2 of your waking hours in life. Social contracts are working here like good days, sick days, acting passive-aggressive, being aggressive-aggressive, co-dependence, joy, empathy, and more. Keeping this mind, the tools of recovery help me perform better on the job with a team.

When responding calmly and kindly to someone's opinion that they shared with you solicited or not, everyone continues to move forward. When frustration bubbles to the top, I've gained skills to use my coping and response filter, which involves pausing when someone is pushing my buttons. I rarely get angry any longer, it's an unnecessary emotion that waste a lot of energy. It's because I don't need to get angry anymore, it's a beautiful thing to take into a professional setting each day.

Yes, I get frustrated, frequently actually because I'm ambitious and driven, and an addict that likes things my way. But my frustration resolves quickly, I move past it because there are more efficient and positive ways to spend the day. I've got people around me who let me talk it out, then we move on. I don't harbor resentments, I don't sit in the negative, I've let it go. No mistake this approach doesn't equate to be a push-over, just the opposite in fact. I've experienced this approach bringing more solutions than anything.

Perfection

My profundity is saying a prayer or meditation out loud like "progress not perfection." I say this a lot; it might go on my cremation urn. Maybe those words could be said when my ashes are illegally scattered somewhere on this earth. If there are some areas in my life I regress, I'm hopeful I'll reset and remind myself to enjoy that moment.

I've experienced and enjoyed improvement and real growth in sobriety. We, humans, are always involved when feelings and facts get all jumbled up. Then the dots connect and whatever I'm struggling with clicks into place.

I've never been a perfectionist, thank goodness, it's one issue I don't have to address. I work on enough things already. But after years in recovery, being sober, doing the work on myself, I mutter these words: "Progress, not perfection today." I'm reasonably sure I'll always believe that's the case for me—just do my best. I'm going to try my best, admit and celebrate my failures, be excited about my successes, and live a life where I feel content about what I'm contributing to the world.

Relax Dude

Relaxing can be hard for me. It was impossible without several drinks before I got sober. In fact, one of the questions I'd posed early in sobriety was how do I have fun and relax? This was a completely foreign concept.

I was numbing with wine, gin, and whiskey to put the world and my emotions on pause. Numbing out everything, distorting how I felt about myself was the way I survived my significant self-hatred. A constant feeling of dread and despair didn't allow me to relax. One day, I thought to myself, "What if life just doesn't get any better?" I started searching for an answer.

I finally had an experience where I realized my relaxation needed some work. I was consulting a few years ago at the National Restaurant Association convention. I was helping one of the Association charities raise awareness and money for a children's education and nutrition program. The brought in several celebrity chefs to talk and take pictures with attendees. My celebrity chef had hosted Restaurant: Impossible, he was gracious, and people adored him. He turned directly to me, and said unsolicited, "Smile! Why do you look so serious? Relax man." I took the advice, and maybe his next show should have been: "Relax Impossible?"

Nowadays I'm still not the best at relaxing but am doing a little better. These experiences of living my life in a way that unsolicited advice can be embraced for how it was intended, to be helpful, is my new normal. The past is remembered but learned from, yet left in the past, where it belongs. There is no one in my head or life echoing any of my ridiculous random thoughts, such as you're an imposter and don't belong. I'm relaxing more, but it's progress, not perfection.

Chapter 24

Survival DNA

IN MY FIRST BOOK IN THE Note to Self-series, 99 lessons, one of the "lessons" I keep re-reading as many times as any: "Feelings are real, but not the facts." I seem to revisit this quite often as a reminder of the lesson I learned when I learned to feel in recovery. This in contrast to numbing myself into oblivion with alcohol. I've committed to a recovery lifestyle, which encompasses rigorous honesty. Honesty which at times feels hard because of fear, but in recovery, it's vital.

It starts with awareness, then enough willingness to be vulnerable. As people, we are built to survive. Survival is reacting to threats, and we all have been born with very primal wiring to address this. The feeling part of our person-architecture is roughly 30% of our overall makeup per Dr. Rick Hanson in the book, Buddha's Brain: The Practical Neuroscience of Happiness, Love & Wisdom. Dr. Hanson breaks down why feeling isn't more natural, why flight or fight or reacting comes naturally without the need for thoughtfulness: 70% survival, 30% feeling. Well, no wonder we do what we sometimes do.

Being Poetry

The tension, sitting across a table with seven looking at me, felt like the start of improv. The minutes ticked. So many unspoken truths, one room, one table, at this very moment, could see it reconcile.

Life great, one transition, maybe change old anew, happy and un. Moments of heal, painful memories, and love because of laughter. Good stories of these ordinary people, recovering.

One moved on, one smiled, and we cried authenticity. Carrying hope that pieces come together again but no. Time moved most by choice, transformed by only time, only felt like it stopped.

Sad, compelling commentary on control and fear, win more than not when power surrenders. This lesson proved, repeatedly, government topples, laws protect, no, and atrocities are recoverable. We fade a distance, yes not forgotten.

Hopeful for growth, change, and fall forward. Every stranger, friend, and blood met, sees again. Resilience and optimism our keystone, getting better, improving. I continue to try—all I can.

Complex Relationships

I'll be the first to admit relationships are complicated when free-willed people are involved. Of course, dynamic and complex because we're making decisions from the information we've maybe or maybe not misinterpreted. I remember having anxiety over relationships since being a young, seven years old. Withdrawing and isolating from others became my coping strategy for dealing with uncomfortable moments.

It's not my default reaction any longer, as much anyway, I've done therapy and recovery from alcoholism, a big difference. I'd categorize myself an extroverted introvert, I am a fan of Carl Jung if you need to know more about personality types. Learning about my personality has been vital for me to understand me. It all takes work to make these situations with relationships work. I've lessened the intensity of my patterns by working to uncomplicate my relationships. My experiences are not that uncommon, family relationships have so many sides and shape to them.

"Courage is not the absence of fear, but the capacity to act despite our fears."

— JOHN McCAIN, U.S. SENATOR

I don't know of one therapist in the late '70s or early '80s in rural farm country, middle Nebraska where I spent my childhood. There could have been some, I sure didn't come across any or anyone sharing how their therapy was helping them. I hope there is many more now, but I don't feel it's changed a lot based on mental health data in rural communities.

It's hard to get healthy with no help. This is when people just give up and resolve themselves not to change, continually uttering the words, "I am just what I am."

Yes, despite what feels comfortable to say to someone or think to we, "relationships have a shelf-life." It was the most discussed and comment-ed lesson in my first book. It resonates with many as it did with me. There are some people we meet, and we've got something in common, and connection. They're interested, but then as everyone adds experience, loss, belief systems, and expectation to the equation, growth happens and increasingly we can move apart. The relationship wasn't bad, but maybe it was unhealthy, and it just needs to conclude. There is just too much to fix with me and us. It's hit the end of its shelf life.

We don't seem to be designed to let go and say goodbye easily. Ending a relationship that's not abusive and toxic, is hard. Even when it needs to stop for safety, it feels hard. It's a battle not to personalize it as a failure. Feelings of failure are usually accompanied by shame, embarrassment, fear, and guilt. These are fear emotions. A societal reaction seems to be, "I'm sorry to hear that." Please stop saying that, it's not helping anyone feel better but you.

Next time don't throw something out without thinking or think-ing or asking how they feel about it. Read the room first, layering your opinions or misplaced empathy doesn't accomplish what's churning in someone's heart.

I'm focused on being gracious yet establishing a bottom line with every relationship worth having. A bottom line is something I won't go past. Remember to love often, love always.

Shelf Life

Yes, "relationships have a shelf-life." It was the most discussed and commented lesson in my first book. It seems to resonate with many as it did with me. There are some people we meet, and we've got something in common, a connection. They're interested, but then as everyone adds experience, loss, belief systems, and expectation we grow, and can grow apart. The relationship wasn't bad, but maybe it was unhealthy for too many years, and it just needs to conclude. There is just too much to fix with me and us.

We don't seem to be designed to let go and say goodbye easily or naturally. Ending a relationship that's not that abusive and that toxic, even then, it's hard not to personalize it as a failure. Feelings of failure are usually accompanied by embarrassment, fear, and guilt. These are more self-conscious emotions. A societal reaction seems to be, "I'm sorry to hear that."

Next time don't throw something out without thinking or asking how they feel about it. Read the room first because layering your opinions or misplaced empathy doesn't accomplish was is likely in one's heart. I'm focused on being gracious yet establishing a bottom line. A bottom line is something I won't go past. Again, relationships can have a shelf-life. That's alright, almost everything in life does. Remember to love often, love always.

Chapter 25

Controlling

WHAT'S IN OUR CONTROL? A QUESTION asked 1000 times gets 997 different answers. Yes, accountability. Yes, clean my side of the street. I hear those dialogs and subscribe to all those tenants. The derailing part of the equation is baggage that needs to be worked through to get to an action plan in place.

A threat of poor outcomes and negative thoughts are ingredients to get me to goals. That's messed up, yet how I think quite a lot. My god, I wonder if these efforts to change only have short-term or zero success at all. It's indeed how I feel sometimes.

Beating myself upon the failure of a goal has become normalized and is accompanied by shame spiraling. This was me my active drinking. We control our actions and interpretations of feelings if healthy. Being healthy could take therapy, meditation, exercise, and medication. There are many ways to be centered and fit in your life. We need to learn to restart without pushing ourselves deeper into a hole.

What to do? I'm figuring this out with everyone else. Feel what you're feeling, be mad, be sad, get out why you're doubting or having to restart repeatedly. Do whatever it takes. But just don't give up until it happens, whatever it is your doing, keep putting one foot in front of another. Say, I just don't want to go to the gym five days a week. It doesn't mean I'm a terrible person; it means I don't want to go to the gym five times. Maybe I'm lazy, maybe my other habits of inactivity are not re-wired yet.

I don't need to bury what I'm thinking about it or guilt myself. Be out, loud, and proud of it. Discuss goals with someone that you can check in with about the process and progress, this little thing, being connected is essential. This is hard for so many of us, but it's an option I hope you figure out how to utilize with a partner, friend, spouse, family, sponsor, pastor, priest, trainer, or therapist.

Act, write down the plan, schedule it into a routine. Make it into your routine. Turn the bad feelings into a good habit. It was difficult to do, but I need a goal to reach, and research supports that working with your habit cycle in mind works. Set short goals. Then commit to a target, guaranteed to achieve if you're able to break down goals and objectives.

It's highly likely you're about self-sabotage and don't even know it, I know I can be left to my own devices. Get one done accomplished, no matter how hard, how simple or how long it takes, and then set the next one.

This isn't about your control, it's about your process and pulling fears apart into small pieces to kick their ass with a process. Yes, you need help. It's hard to ask for this, but it's part of a program to improve. An essential part.

Within Our Power

My "power." I toggle back and forth on what this term means to me. If this is more about control and fear versus empowerment and freedom, then I need to keep thinking about it.

Two definitions of power:
a) The ability to do something or act in a way, primarily as a faculty or quality. Ex. "the power of speech."
b) The capacity or ability to direct or influence the behavior of others or the course of events. Ex. "she had me under her power."

The 'a' definition I feel pretty good about, I could substitute "live" for "act"; it feels like it should be there. 'b' is where I am hesitant about. It feels like manipulation. Obviously, I'm layering my experience on the top of these definitions. Now if I substituted "behavior of me" and "course of my life" then yes, I've accepted how power can be a healthy term in recovery.

We do learn skills as we recover from addiction first—then we recovery from life next. That the choice to not pick up that first drink or drug is my first line of defense! Doing the next right thing if my lifestyle defense. I suppose it was not as cut and dried for some; not all our security for staying sober will be the same. One misconception is one size fits all with addiction, but that is not the case.

I never want to appear to diminish harm reduction as a solution or drinking management. There is a place for any type of recovery that saves people's lives, period. Keep trying to recover, however, you need to do it.

Chapter 26

Bullying

I AM TRYING TO REMEMBER WHAT intimidated felt like as a kid. It's a clear memory of these feelings, because they're so significant. My world was constantly avoiding being verbally beaten down growing up, constant intimidation. There is no way or need to sugar coat it.

Having older cousins in school for me was a blessing because the know bullies felt they might be held accountable for anything too outlandish with me as an underclassman. I know what started out as being teased for some turned into harassment for others—traumatizing events that impacted the rest of their lives. I didn't have that much of this in school.

It happens in hallways, locker rooms, sports fields, and everywhere else there is more than a single person. Bullying has been one of the leading causes of adolescent suicide in recent years. It's likely been this way for quite some time but was under reported. Social media has provided more range and frequency to the bullying, also known as cyberbullying.[1]

My older cousins around the school presented that psychology security that no one wants to get zapped by, again I guess, I was lucky. But there many who were not. They got teased to terrorized about their appearance to some different behavior. It was helpful to someone older keeping an eye out for me. I got teased but usually by those protecting me. They were likely watching out for me a lot more than I realized. Most kids don't have the option of the family looking out for them. Which I feel is a prevalent public health crisis in the U.S., which I learned first-hand while helping my friend Angela Maiers[2] at a school district in Texas a few years ago.

Angela is a world-renowned author, entrepreneur, international keynote speaker, and educator, whose transformative message of the importance of mattering has the power to unleash the genius in us all. Her message is centered around "everyone matters, you matter." When you witness Angela being approached by children who wanted or have attempted suicide, we've got a tragic public health crisis on top of us.

Looking back at my growing up in a small school, a small community where everyone knows everybody. It was forced transparency, at least it felt this way. This small community made the fear worse, it wasn't a great place to share how drowning you feel each day. How unsettled and out of place you think, in every single circumstance. It felt like we were on an island, in rural America, and I was drowning before I touched the water. My escaping from the island, staying with this metaphor was numbing myself to a blackout as a 15-year-old.

Then I found alcohol and staying drunk, even though the conse-quences could be severe, it was still a better option. Honestly, I don't remember if we really had a guidance counselor, I wouldn't have talked to them anyway, I was too fearful. There was a lot of bullying and intimi-dation by older boys and girls in my school years.

The younger kids had it bad in junior high and high school based on what little I remember and were told. People felt ostracized and shutout on purpose, very mean girl cliché scenarios with the males and females both. This isolation technique, especially by groups of people are power-fully deviant and devastating to someone young, just trying to go to school.

Isolation and lack of connection are elements that lead us addicts and anyone cycling through any mental health episode to substance use, self-harm, and suicide. It compounds what kids are experiencing at home and within themselves-depression, anxiety, or other disorders.

We must do more to eliminate isolation, promote and support a connection. Teachers and kids need to be as much of this solution at school as parents do at home.

Ask someone you know or don't, what happened today, and how are they feeling? They are questions that take practice and can be hard, but they're necessary questions to ask, please join me in being part of the solution.

Eliminating the negative, be positive, stand up for what is kind and the next right thing to do. I can't go back in time and do this, I didn't know how. I'm so sorry for those I could have but didn't defend or support when these things happened.

Back then years ago, we had nothing more than face-to-face to communicate. Today, there are more ways to communicate which makes cyberbullying 24/7 with digital devices, BUT we also have an equal opportunity to protect and support those in need and crisis, 24/7. The positivity and message of everyone matters will always win. Please join me in trying much harder to be there.

> *"When I say to you from the bottom of my heart: YOU MATTER, I say this not to inspire you or make you feel better about yourself."*
>
> — ANGELA MAIERS, AUTHOR, EDUCATOR & SPEAKER

All Alone

Isolation is powerful and cruel, when others do this to you as a child, and equally bad when you learn to self-impose this on yourself in childhood well into adulthood.

What I'd do differently in reflection is stand up, help someone be a voice by finding my voice to help, speaking out more frequently and loudly for those who didn't feel they could. We've all felt this way in one situation or another. These kids, my peers felt alone with no backup or support, very little hope. Just like I did, we're the same.

I was luckier in this situation, people kept an eye open for me, I had a safety net most of the life, no idea why other than I'm able to use the grace I've shown to share a message of recovery with others.

What I remember most clearly was one specific age of kids, an unhappy lot of boys. They were the terrorizers, name-callers, physical and emotional abusers back then, I witnessed this and experienced directly. No one was completely immune from this group. I wasn't as open to being physically bullied because I was a bigger kid than average back then, this time it worked in my favor. These boys were cowards, they went after who was most vulnerable, or the most obvious vulnerabilities.

With me they stuck with an emotional abuse approach, me being overweight, more significant than most everyone for my age they went after me with a crash nickname that referenced being fat. I was called by the group and others, 'Butch.' I fucking hated it and hated them. That's not the case any longer, I've reconciled others behavior and my hate for them to the fact they were unhappy, I don't know why they were this way. They could have been bullied, abused, and battling with their mental health, all things I don't know. I've chosen to open that space to positive and forgive.

The nickname was derived after a business owner in town—a guy who could literally lift a motor out of a car by himself. He was a big dude, quiet but as strong as a powerful bull. Toward me, it wasn't meant as a compliment.

A couple years into high school, I hit my limit on the nickname thing, I started pushing back, enough that they knew I wouldn't always take it. End of the day, my father was exponentially more intimidating than these yahoos. Ultimately, they graduated, and it stopped because I wouldn't tolerate it from peers. I was reasonably quick to share my thoughts when someone would use the nickname. My stock response was, "go fuck yourself," not my name. Some of the reasons people love college so much, life can restart in some ways, like leaving nicknames behind.

In thinking about those years, I was starting to drink to escape. I was also getting more competitive in sports, this ended up being another place I was finding my voice more and more. The bullies weren't that much bigger than me, so I'd deliver an occasional hit on the football field that made me, and my peers feel a little vindicated. Look, I don't recommend this as your vindication, but if it's the best you can do for yourself at that time, you do it. I've changed so much, I don't I think this way today, life isn't about searching for retribution, it's about courage with character. I would communicate such as a different message today, to this group than back then.

For kids today, I hope they find someone to confide, and trust with your story, to get help and support. We're out there, please keep asking until it happens. I know it's hard, I still remember and always will. You matter your part of changing the world with positivity, we don't want to lose you. This period in my life, with all my internal chaos and unsettled home life, this bullying, beat up my self-image quite a lot. Being kind is an example of being a positive steward of good will in this world.

It genuinely feels like I was being watched over with grace my entire life. Something has kept me alive to finally heal by finding recovery, to then use my experience to help others find a way to save their lives. I don't remember bullying anyone, but if I did, I'm sorry and as apologetic as I can possibly be so many years later. It was wrong, no excuses, it was wrong.

Today, I'm committed to standing up for those who are struggling to do it for themselves. Addiction is vicious and complex, much like other chronic and fatal diseases. I stand up for those battling addiction, getting bullied, and isolating others as outsiders. We're all weirdos, unique, creative, eclectic, whatever because we're also fascinating.

Those in that negative cycle of diminishing those around them, are likely confined to obscurity themselves. Please, I'm hoping you'll stand up for yourself, and many others will stand up and be the voices for those who don't, won't, or can't stand up for whatever reason. Many of us have been terrified and alone. You're not alone; we're here for you, together we have tremendous strength and hope.

Ninety Days

I've experienced and discussed many times, several different ways that individuals get started in recovery. It's very similar and different, every single time. Most are chasing to change how they feel, numbing an indescribable pain from the trauma of some type, not always but often. They're now down the road, a few years of drinking, or using whatever you're doing, the invisible line is crossed and now your physically dependent on a substance to feel normal, each day, then each hour, then altogether.

Most of us don't arrive at recovery happy and healthy. No one blows out the candles in the birthday cake wishing to grow up to be an addict. But our best efforts at managing our life got us to the starting point of recovery. No ever woke up one morning, then rolled up to a basement of a dilapidated church to drink horrific coffee and smoke cheap cigarettes with a but of alcoholics and drug addicts at the nightly A.A meeting. Was their life fulfilling and peaceful as they battled addiction, no it was not.

It's a real nightmare that you're utterly awake in your own life. We are lost, spiraling in pain, in trouble from a combination of things, it's raw for the first 90 days. For most of us, 90 days is more sobriety than we've had for several years. If you're a lucky one, recovery somehow finds you before you kill someone or yourself. I absolutely felt more at home in that church basement drinking wonderfully bad coffee with a room full of strangers that I knew every one of their stories because they were me, I was them.

Thank goodness, the recovery conversation is becoming more mainstream. You're likely to have some exposure, education, or experience with a form of recovery group support program, 12-step, faith-based, harm-reduction, treatment (in or outpatient). You've heard about it or know someone who's been involved with it.

The initial 90 days of sobriety is about experiencing a new routine while working the alcohol and drugs physically out of your system. You've restarted your emotional development that generally stopped when you started using, whether 11 or 18 years old. Note that drugs can take much longer than 90 days to get entirely out of your system physically, keep that in mind. The same but different but the same.

"We will love you until you love yourself enough to care."
— A.A. CATHY

Chapter 27

Show Up

TAKE TO HEART PLEASE, 90 MEETINGS in 90 days, per several of the anonymous support group programs, find therapy several times, more exercise of any kind, or combination of all of these. Make sure to do something related to getting sober each day for yourself.

Those who want to help, they aren't going to be there all the time, do your best to help yourself each day. These means don't drink or use any substances; if you do use, tell some you did, be honest then start over. It happens to more than not. You're at the front end of retraining your brain, body, and spirit in somewhat that order. It needs repetition, it doesn't know what you're asking it to do when you start. A key is asking for help, this was incredibly hard for me, still is sometimes. I'd learned to survive, I saw people living without help my whole life. Yes, they weren't happy or peaceful, but I didn't know what those things were quite yet. Yes, this is hard, best and hardest thing you'll ever do.

Your recovery family all know this, but it's what we've got to do to save our lives. Try walking into a 12-step meeting, therapy, treatment program, etc. Just keep trying, keep walking into situations to get you better. If you don't "show up" in some way, somewhere, it's impossible for recovery to start.

Exercise

Your body is processing chemicals, alcohol or drugs and god only knows what else you've put in your body, I would know. Exercise will help your body to reset the usual old way it processed what was put into it. Rewiring how your brain and general body work together is essential, if not somewhat required to get recovery completely. We exercise our bodies to release chemicals called endorphins. These endorphins interact with the receptors in our brains that reduce our perceptions of pain. Endorphins also trigger a positive feeling in the body, like that we all chased from substances on natural to your body. This information was pulled from WebMD and some other medical website that I couldn't remember where.

I work on being active daily, I've got to be active, I want to be active but seem to come up short. My entire life I've battled being fit, I've been in great shape physically but emotional was in sync, so I didn't continue. I quit, then I have to be honest and start over, as many times as it takes. This not being very fit, impacts me and those around me, how I feel, how I think and what I do each day. I'm not going to stop trying and asked for help. It has been shared that I need to exercise 150 minutes per week minimum, didn't know that. I took a buddy on being a workout accountability partner, again, grace seems to keep finding me for a reason. I'm thankful and do my best today.

The Food

Your eating hasn't likely been the healthiest when you walk into treatment or recovery where you start; you could even have triggers for using from food. In clinical settings, if you enter treatment one of the first things covered in intake is a recent history of consumption of food.

"No specific diets are best for alcoholics and addicts in early recovery," Kane-Davidson, and other experts wrote. "But the optimal eating regimen for people trying to kick their alcohol and drug habits do share some common elements with many of the eating plans that perform well on U.S News' annual Best Diets rankings. An optimal plan emphasizes protein from fish, poultry and lean meat, fresh vegetables and fruit, legumes and whole-grain bread and cereals." If you're a vegetarian or vegan adjust accordingly, it's still the same concept.

Relationshipping

Everyone in and out of recovery is searching for meaningful connections, relationships that make you feel good, supported, and basically like a better person. That is a good partnership when this happens, in short, fulfilled. Early in recovery, our emotions are so raw, to say the least. We're new to many emotional unknowns in sobriety, and it's going to take a while to unpack the bags. Reality is we arrive at the sober party with our many, many emotional blackholes learned from using substances and people for years. To be honest with yourself about what's ahead, you've got a chance to get healthy and have a good life.

Making room for another person in your life is as natural as it might feel because you're feeling better, life is getting better. It's time to be cautious and careful, you're still sick when you're early in sobriety. You want some companionship, and fewer things are blowing up these days, of course, we want to date. Keeping in mind, you've immersed in recovery, early sobriety with lots of sick people, we've been there. It's why we're recovering. We take a while to get healthier, healthy enough to move back into the relationship stage of living. In sobriety you learn how to live your life, communicate, set boundaries for you and others, all the things that stopped being learned when you started using drugs and alcohol.

Well, don't jump into being in like or love, get it a little while. Just focus on yourself in early sobriety, for the first six months. I've always heard it takes 1-year in recovery for every 3-years of using to learn how to learn to live a life, you fall in love with living. You're rehabbing your entire life, so don't rush into something too soon.

For those in a relationship, the living ratio I used: 1-year single to

4-years in the relationship. Example, 15-year partnership ends, divide by 15 by 4, that's how I long I'd work to clean up my side of the emotional street. These unhealthy patterns are carried over from childhood to adulthood into relationships. You've likely been in active addiction in adulthood in that old relationship, and you need some time to fix things. Even after being in recovery, fix your stuff before you carry it right to the next one.

Is this easy? Of course not, but it's what will keep you sober and happier long-term when your relationship patterns are healthier. There are excellent reasons to limit new romantic relationships and other significant life decisions for the first 12 months, main is your head isn't clear. You're needing to react to all the things you're trying to fix in your life. The time provides you with space and time to learn new tools to help you. Find others who can share how they handled it and clear your body and mind from substances first. If the relationship is dangerous or abusive, you'll need to act, protect yourself, whatever it takes. Please ask someone for help, keep praying, keep asking someone will be there.

Routine

Putting together consistent activity each day was one of the most important parts of my early recovery. It allowed me to "not think about things." Example, wake up, think a positive thought, say a prayer that I tailored for me, then meditate for a couple of minutes. 10-years later, I do this every single day, then I make the bed. It helped me to rewire my brain, I start accomplishing things, completing tasks I've committed each day before I even think about it.

Every person in early recovery questions being "bored," and is this my boring life until I die someday. A routine helps take over-thinking out of my loop, I just act. Don't worry about excitement like police cars, electricity being shut-off, and being pulled into a fight with a bunch of other drunk people. By the way, there is a "misery back guarantee" if you don't like being sober.

Connection

Loneliness has been identified as a leading public health issue in 2018. In addiction recovery, connection with others is an essential part of healing, a part of learning how to trust, relate to, and cope with others in our sober family. An American Psychological Association study found that lonely people are at a higher risk for premature death, combine that will drinking whiskey and using crystal meth, I'd say the risk goes up even more. Let's connect and be sober together. It's a better life.

Chapter 28

Mental Health

75% OF ALCOHOLICS ARE SUFFERING FROM more than alcoholism, whether it be depression, PTS, bipolar disorder, or a litany of the conditions. Stopping drinking and using will start to eliminate distortion of your reality and present more accurate visibility into what your options might be.

The National Bureau of Economic Research (NBER) reports that there is a definite connection between mental illness and the use of addictive substances. Individuals with existing mental illness consume roughly 38 percent of all alcohol, 44 percent of all cocaine, and 40 percent of all cigarettes. Furthermore, the people who have ever experienced mental illness consume about 69 percent of all the alcohol, 84 percent of all the cocaine, and 68 percent of all cigarettes.

Everyone knows someone impacted by using drugs and alcohol. Don't stay out of the conversation any longer.

Therapy

After I stopped drinking, I experienced a mix of people in recovery willing to talk about therapy work they'd done for every reason you and I could think of and more. I'm a firm believer that if you want to get sober and pursue sustainable recovery, you need help other than 12-step support groups.

There is a complex and layered person looking back at us in the mirror each day. The human condition is questioning and working on past experiences from all sorts of memories and trauma. Trauma could be micro to significantly tragic and complex; there could be one or many events involved in the emotional injury.

What I have learned from therapy is it could be a combination of emotional and possibly physical wounds—my interpretation of trauma. In recovery, I've started to unpack events, emotions, and understandings of why I act and feel how I do today. How and what I do with all these feelings is vastly different from when I first entered recovery. This is because I've done a ton of 12-step, therapy, and meditation work. It's what I had to do for improvement, your path could be different.

Won't Keep It

You hear in recovery almost day 1: Do service work, help a support group, your church, food pantry or whatever to give back and be of service. It was presented in context for me to give back to a 12-step group I was participating. They suggested I make coffee, clean up after meetings, sweep, and dump ashtrays if it's a meeting that you can smoke. I remember, smoking permitted A.A. meetings; I only went a few times. It was quite the experience as most old A.A. rooms don't ventilate well. As the meeting progressed, a cloud would get thicker from smoke and start to go lower and lower. It was something else.

Anyway, the point was to help clean up, give back and be of service to the group, to people, get out of my head for a bit and do something that wasn't about me (selfless). As they say, you must give it away to keep it. You must continue to provide service, or you might end up using in your head first, then actually believe it's a good idea. That's how it happens. It sneaks back in, long before a drink or drug happens. Go sign up to volunteer, do something that you don't expect anything from but a good feeling for doing it.

Chapter 29

Back Then

So many drinks in 27 years of chasing that feeling of relief, the experience with early drinking. Early drinking was an escape or was it, I'm not sure. The escapism is what worked for most when they very first started drinking. Reflecting on this, it was more about belonging, being part of something. It was an act to find acceptance, the question still begs for an answer, is this stem from my initial feeling of unknowing abandon and detachment because of my adoption.

This book is focused more on my total addiction recovery, which is more than just alcohol. It was time to tell more about my whole story, and I've decided to share all my experiences. I started drugs in 1987 or 88', brushed with an overdose in 1992, started to try quitting drugs then and finally did in 1996, then 14 years long years later, alcohol in 2010

The coldest I remember growing up in Nebraska was 48 degrees below zero wind-chill. I mean damn cold there, it was a dangerous cold. There were bottles under every seat and in every barn in the Midwest, whiskey or schnapps. I started consuming the "candy cane drink" early and as often as I could get away with it, a weird feeling, I liked it at first because I didn't know any better, next out of choice to change me.

Many years of self-medicating ended up becoming my routine, wake up, open my eyes, breathe, want not to feel anything "normal." I was just like millions of others who are struggling with how they survive in the world, but addicts go deeper, struggling with how we feel others want us to behave, act, be. There is no escape until we change our thinking.

I'm not unique. In recovery, I'm graced to hear people's stories about the complexity of addiction and trauma, recovery and relapse, and hope-fully—if they survive—recovery again. I hear people give their lives back after incredible experiences.

Decompress

How do you decompress after a long and trying week, my always question? I was tired, my brain and body were exhausted, when I got home and wandered around a few rooms of our home. Finally, my wife pointed out that I was just wandering around. This got me thinking: Did I want to decompress, take a nap, take a walk, or what. Do most people after a full day wish to escape or just to slow things down to focus on something that allows them to quiet their mind and soul for a few minutes calmly. Do most people think this way? Yes, we do. It's called calming or relaxing.

7 of 10 people hate their job in the U.S., they'd walk out today if they didn't face financial insecurity. 70% hate the work they do 9 hours per day. That can't be good for productivity and loyalty. That is staggering but not that surprising based on what I see each day, the comments shared without caring what their co-workers or I think.

I'm hearing thoughts bouncing off cubicles, "I just want to survive what I do for today." Maybe I'll get lucky, and get hurt, they pay me, I never have to come back to this job. These are real thoughts that people say out loud. We've all had jobs that we didn't like but couldn't afford to quit. This is where meditation before, during, and after the day wraps up is lovely. It's a wellness oasis in your mind, it's mobile, and you deserve it.

My theory is intentional meditation, and calming practices to quiet your mind could literally change your life, give you more peace and years on this earth. Meditation and positive mantras have become essential tools for me. I've learned all of these in recovery from substances. If you're not headed to recovery anytime soon, learn how to meditate, that's a great place to start for everyone.

Yoga

It wasn't until two years into sobriety. I met some lovely people, caring souls, who shared what they knew about meditation, breathwork and expanding my life within me. It changed my life forever. I enjoy using what they and others have shared with me, every single day to center me and my world around me. It helps me deal with what is outside, which again helps me deal with what is on the inside.

All these calming practices are inexpensive and available even when your mobile gives us. Please, give it a try for 30 seconds of meditation. Close your eyes, take a deep breath for 8 seconds, while saying please, then exhale for 7 seconds, while saying thank you, do these four times. Guess what, you just meditated. You did a great job.

Back to today, I was tired and needed something funny, so I fired up a comedy with Amy Schumer. It worked for me, I felt better. These actors deliver stories to entertain us, that was my escape, my meditation of a certain kind. Before sobriety, I starkly remember escaping that tiredness by drowning in alcohol. Much gratitude today and thanks Schumer for a healthy way to revive and recharge my soul, and my life.

Chapter 30

Waking Up

HUMAN BEINGS ARE INCREDIBLY RESILIENT AND designed for survival. I've mentioned this several times, but it was vital for me to learn this. This survival default is part of our support system that helps rationalize how low our standard of happiness and joy can go. I mean the bar is lowered to unthinkable levels of what "a good day" ends up being. When waking up in a place you recognize, alone, with all your stuff is a great day, you have some upside at a good day.

People with a substance dependency are six times more likely to complete suicide, with 33% of these suicides being done under the influence a drug (alcohol, oxycodone or heroin). When life has progressed in a downward in the grips of active addiction, many are just surprised and happy enough they woke up again. Just a little thing like being alive and not waking up covered in vomit is something to be grateful, when not sober. What's interesting is many at the lowest points of addiction, not waking would be equally as good, if not a better option. Thankfully many of us get another day and another chance.

This was a challenging section for me to write because it brought up memories from the past, what feels like a long time ago but was less than 10-years ago. That feeling of just wanting, begging everything to stop. I wanted me to stop my life. What a simply complicated thing to think. Since that day, I can empathize and understand what those reading my book are feeling.

It's alright, I had the same thoughts at various times about others "giving up," not trying something else, taking the easy way out. All those thoughts are what people think, let's be honest, honest. I've had these thoughts and been that person so disillusioned, desperate and hopeless that suicide might be the best answer. I'm not worth being here. Honestly, I never thought I'd ever considered suicide until that day, I did think about it.

It was another moment of grace, that day I feel fortunate to have been in recovery when this happened. I talked to someone about these thoughts. He asked the question that always needs to ask first, "Do you want to do it is that your plan"? My answer was no, it was just a thought that made it to the surface. He shared how important it was to remember, I immediately ask for help and I talked to someone. Many in recovery experience this situation, get help, talk to someone right away, no matter what. We need you, we everyone, we're all worth it and matter to this world.

Normalize Recovery

It feels good year by year, being part of the recovery community. Whether it's a connection through a loved one or you are in treatment. Transitions into what I'd refer to as a typical conversation about healing from a complex disorder are happening more frequently. It was 1895 when imprisonment in the U.S. was likely for a common defective, referred to as an alcoholic, so discussing your dependency freely for alcohol or drugs wasn't advisable.

If many found out your dependence, all would be lost in society, an outcast. Fast forward to 1935 when you might get fired and institutionalized in a hospital or mental asylum for your issues with alcohol. Well, present day, the conversation isn't backrooms, church basements, or in the same shadow that led you into addiction treatment. Today is about healing, getting better and have a life you're excited about living.

Learn to Respond

We are wired to react, finish thoughts, and immediately fix things. Well, those are good things in certain situations, like being chased by a bear or wolf. They are both scary.

In day-to-day life reacting to everything will lead to uninformed decisions because you don't have enough information. This is where learning the skill of responding comes into the light. I don't feel we're born with this. I think it's starting to develop around 7-years old, about the time we're beginning to figure ourselves out. Since being in recovery from addiction, I've learned how much of a discrepancy I have with emotional coping tools. Before starting recovery, the gaps in how I processed feelings and information were constantly raging with emotional highs and lows, I operated in constant stress.

These thoughts go through a filter in my head and heart now. These happen in the blink of an eye because I've practiced, I exercise these tools every day. This exercise is supported by meditation, group recovery meetings, and some for activity and movement.

Chapter 31

Be the Heavy

Today, life is more satisfying, filled with challenge and happiness. After many years in recovery from alcoholism, I'm asking similar questions of myself that I was asked throughout my drinking and using years. Issues such as you're always going to be big (overweight), why does it matter, and why am I feeling out of control. I struggle to find an answer in this one area of my life, managing fitness, and whole health recovery. This is a part of my life I have struggled with since age 6-years old. I've had some fitness successes like an alcoholic or addict with periods of not using, temporary health recovery, my food sobriety. Then a workout is skipped, an extra couple pieces of pizza or a late-night burger starts the spiral again.

This mental obsession over my weight was happening years before I started drinking and using drugs as a teenager. It goes way back deep into childhood, one I'm yet to understand. I'm still a work in progress. Part of sharing what is going on with me helps me. What I'm trying to change is ending the stigma and emotional turmoil internalized if one is significantly overweight. I know, the same can happen for anyone dealing with body image issue.

Obese (having excessive body fat) is hard to say but it's a clinical term and sure as hell is better than blubbery, stocky, chubby, fat, fleshy, plump, portly, pudgy, roly-poly, rotund, or tubby. These names that anyone who's been overweight have endured in their lifetime are fucking brutal to hear. They are not funny, they're equally painful and damaging as most of the stigmatizing terms directed toward the various people associated with many health conditions.

Stop using these words, use someone's name not how they look. It's called person first language, you'll learn this if you get Mental Health First Aid certified. Yes, it takes work to unlearn these normalized parts of our language, but it's a kinder path. In context, it's no different than any other stigmatizing descriptions, words, and names that are thrown around each day. They're unnecessary to communicate effectively. Please work on being part of the difference by stopping the stigmatizing language.

Say something nice, there is a start. These are good people who could be drowning in shame, insecurity, and pain on the outside for all to see, and comment about. It's not everybody that feels this way, it's still a lot. This is how I think about it at times.

I don't want to struggle my entire life with a fitness issue. If I'm able to bring awareness to how I'm rewiring my behaviors and lifestyle to support being healthier, then I save myself by sharing with others about my story, which is being written, today. I'm ready to get super honest about this one topic, I fear more than anything, literally anything. Just like recovery from alcohol and drugs, I had to hit my bottom. Maybe not the bottom but a point that felt dark enough that I didn't know if I'd find the light again. That was my bottom.

I'm there, and I just seem to fail at sustaining my fitness long-term. My life is good except for this one area, I am not being successful here. Part of any recovery program is working on my emotional health in concert with physical and spiritual health. In the spirit of my whole person approach here I'm not going to fear this fitness thing any longer; I'm willing, hopeful, asking for help, and working to change how I think first, then how I act.

Chapter 32

Save Lives

THERE ARE SO MANY PATHS TO recovery different than the most commonly known 12-step support program, Alcohol Anonymous (A.A.). I'm an active member of A.A., it's the program I used to get sober. It's been my path to recovery, but I'm also quick to challenge anyone who believes this is the only way to heal. We can't be rigid with ways to save people's lives.

There are other programs people utilize to get sober or manage their life back into control. Many have been able to achieve and stay sober using those programs just like A.A.

Based on my experience, I'd work to find something that provides structure for a recovery program, and that's based on the whole person. It would be good, in my opinion, if it's a matrix-like structure with only a couple of people at the top, keep all very accessible. There are a lot of sick people trying to get better out there, starting programs, possibly even with good one with pure and just motives in the beginning, with some power might not end up there. I'm not endorsing any plans or treatments, negative or positive. Here are some other than A.A. support group programs out there, SMART Recovery, Refuge Recovery, and Celebrate Recovery. I know there are more, these are just a few.

Other Treatment

I'm open to about any emotional treatment that doesn't involve snakes, glass or fire, those are my trio that would cause additional pause and consideration. Healing comes in all forms though. There have been emotional healing practices being used long before WebMD, long before Christ rose, long before many of the conquerors where conquering.

The first time I attempted breathwork meditation, I was excited for something unusual to happen, a breakthrough, an experience. Where is my white light, I gave it my all; it was my best effort. Not much arrived for me, I was able to recognize calming, which was great but not the big stuff.

Fast forward, 6-years later, I was in Hollywood, CA for a small recovery retreat with 20 or so other people. Most were attending to talk about writing books on healing and recovery, exploring writing, and marketing as a recovery author. I didn't know a single person attending this retreat and had traveled from Kansas City, Missouri to L.A. The event was hosted by Anna David, a New York Times best-selling author, and Ryan Hampton, recovery advocate and author.

The weekend started awkwardly for me because I didn't know anyone, I'm an introvert who acts extroverted, so I started jumping into conversations. In the end, we were all in recovery, so that common thread comforted my pangs of anxiety. Thank God I stuck around and started to get to know the people. Being in a safe place maybe was a significant variable for what happened. Something transcendent occurred with my racing mind, it was just meant to happen this day.

We had a breathwork meditation in a room with 20 people in recovery. It was cool and a first for me, only slightly overwhelming. I started a breathing cadence that was slow and deep, music playing in the background and the quiet, steady voice from our session leader. I don't remember as much about the before versus the after. We started to speed up and shorten our breathing cadence, very standard breathwork, I'm sort of guessing at this assumption. The session leader warned us that we could get light-headed or hyperventilate to pay attention to that and stop whenever we needed to make sure we stayed safe. I like that.

A shorter, quicker breathing cadence, with my hands on my stomach and chest, lying flat on my back. The next instruction was to think about something. At this point, my memory of specifics gets a little blurry. I started thinking about a biological father I'd never met and didn't know. As I shared in this book several times, a significant event in my life was my adoption at two days old in Redwood City, California.

I'd never met or know anything about my bio-father, never gave him much thought. It was important, I thought anyway. It's something I was interested in, but I had not actively sought that information. I eventually met my birth mother and sisters but nothing on the birth father.

Well, in this meditation session I got focused on him. I didn't know his name, and never even saw his face, but he was all I could think about. I got furious at him for dismissing me and my life. I was entirely consumed with it briefly until it turned to sadness, feeling abandoned. I was regressing through my grief when I was born, that is what I felt happened.

It was an experience that will impact me in my entire life. It's already resulted in healing and my moving forward from something unconscious to me. I had no idea it was holding any space in my spirit. I started to cry, weeping and asking why he didn't care, and why I was nothing to him. Then I immediately found forgiveness. I let go of the anger and shame of not being acknowledged almost 50 years ago. It was an experience that opened my life to more, considerably more than this experience. I want to thank our breathwork leader and those attending for being part of the healing process.

Since the session, I've opened to exploring more who this stranger in my life might be. I've asked more questions about him and completed a commonly known DNA test to see the other 50% of my ancestry that was unknown to me. I learned that I'm Irish, German, and Scandinavian, which I didn't know. If I'm sincere, I was a little disappointed. The science has spoken, I'm very Northern European. Nothing much else but that's OK, I finally know who I am in addition to who my biological father and family are.

Friends

Visiting with my friend Dr. Howard Liu recently, I've decided to include a few thoughts on how important these moments are for me. Connecting with people, whenever this happens, please embrace it for everything you possibly can for these are special moments in time and your life.

We'd been connected through Twitter then formally introduced by a childhood family friend who worked with Howard, note that we live in different cities. It started out old school by scheduling an introduction call of which we hit it off and visited about lots of things background, jobs, families. Then continued to follow each other, sharing various content typically about mental health, health recovery, and life. This is how you make friends in our digital era-shared interest, likeability, and investing time in getting to know each other. It's not that different than the traditional method. Both have busy lives with busy families; I am thankful we get a few minutes to catch up.

Howard and I get about 30-45 minutes in person once a year while attending a conference on behavioral health, hopefully, more in the future, which I said last year but I mean it this year. Our topics range from how to live a more balanced life, how to prioritize all the fantastic things we want to do, changing since we last talked, and ultimately how much we both love the conference. I don't know the science behind, "picking up where you left off last time and not miss a beat" but we do. The time together concludes, my head and a heart are full, and my soul feels a little better. I am grateful that I have a few of these friends scattered throughout the country and world. Take those extra moments if possible, to share some time, it's a gift to yourself.

Chapter 33

Wrapping Up

T EN YEARS INTO MY RECOVERY, I discover how much I dislike being uncomfortable. I'm reminded how much I need to be in some amount of emotional or spiritual discomfort. This seems to push me to figure out other ways to do things. It's practicing expansion and contraction for me; it's growth. It can be frightening at times because you're opening a door you see only darkness until you get it open enough. Then you learn more about what is in front of you in that new place.

I'm excited you honored me and those in recovery by investing your time and money to read this book and think about healing. Thank you. Remember you don't have to be alone, ever again. We're a big recovery family that has our arms open. Be kind to yourself and others, start your day with a please, and end it with a thank you.

Be Willing,

Bryan Wempen
www.bryanwempen.com
info@bryanwempen.com

Available Resources

SAMHSA's National Helpline
Phone: 800-662-4357
Hours: 24/7

NCADD Hope Line
Phone: 800-622-2255
Hours: 24/7

National Suicide Prevention Lifeline
Phone: 800-273-8255
Hours: 24/7

The Trevor Lifeline (LGBTQ+)
Phone: 866-488-7386
Hours: 24/7

U.S. Department of Veterans Affairs Veterans Crisis Line
Phone: 800-273-8255
Hours: 24/7

National Domestic Violence Hotline
Phone: 800-799-7233
Hours: 24/7

Notes and References

Part One

p. 13

"Alcohol Use Disorder," Symptoms and Causes, Mayo Clinic, last modified July 11, 2018, https://www.mayoclinic.org/diseases-conditions/alcohol-use-disorder/symptoms-causes/syc-20369243.

p. 14

It was the first year the data supported that drug overdoses are more lethal than auto accidents.

"Drug Overdoses are Leading Cause of Death for those under 50," Counseling Keys by Kimberly Key, Psychology Today, November 1, 2017, https://www.psychologytoday.com/us/blog/counseling-keys/201711/drug-overdoses-are-leading-cause-death-those-under-50.

Chapter 2. Our Addiction

p. 21

What group is substance-use-disorder is impacting the most? The numbers of deaths and unreported use of alcohol and drugs are skyrocketing with a much older age group.

"Illicit Drug Use," Nationwide Trends, National Institute on Drug Abuse, last updated June, 2015, https://www.drugabuse.gov/publications/drugfacts/nationwide-trends.

p. 21

This signals a public health crisis with addiction is reaching across all age, race, and gender groups. As a reference point, addicts of any kind represent 15% of the U.S. workforce, 20% of the adult U.S. population, and 80% of those diagnosed with a mental health disorder in the United States.

"4 Ways Leaders Can Improver Mental Health In The Workplace," Leadership: Editor's Pick, Forbes Media LLC, October 10, 2018, https://www.forbes.com/sites/nazbeheshti/2018/10/10/4-ways-leaders-can-improve-mental-health-in-the-workplace/#15b3c1c53937.

p. 22

It is my responsibility to continue to carry this message to the 1 in 5 Americans who will experience bouts with substance use disorder each year.

"Prevalence of Mental Illness," Mental Health By The Numbers, National Alliance on Mental Illness, retrieved October 27, 2015, https://www.nami.org/Learn-More/Mental-Health-By-the-Numbers.

p. 22

An estimated 88,000 people (approximately 62,000 men and 26,000 women) die from alcohol-related causes annually, making alcohol the third leading preventable cause of death in the United States. The first is tobacco, and the second is poor diet and physical inactivity.

"Alcohol-Related Deaths," Alcohol Facts and Statistics, National Institute on Alcohol Abuse and Alcoholism, updated August, 2018, https://www.niaaa.nih.gov/alcohol-health/overview-alcohol-consumption/alcohol-facts-and-statistics.

p. 23

In 2014, alcohol-impaired driving fatalities accounted for 9,967 deaths (31 percent of overall driving fatalities).

"Alcohol-Impaired Driving," Traffic Safety Facts: 2014 Data, National Highway Traffic Safety Administration, last modified December, 2015, https://crashstats.nhtsa.dot.gov/Api/Public/ViewPublication/812231.

Chapter 5. My Early Story

p. 31

Private adoption in California with attorneys could be thousands of dollars in 1969, it's not money my new parents had. In fact, $2,000 in 1969 is equivalent to $13,717 in 20198.

"$2,000 in 1969 → 2019 | Inflation Calculator." U.S. Official Inflation Data, Alioth Finance, 31 Mar. 2019, https://www.officialdata.org/us/inflation/1969?amount=2000.

Chapter 6. Next Moves

p. 44

Note, not everyone who gets adopted is impacted by the separation at the birth the same way. The research supports a significant correlation between adoption and considerably higher addiction cases, much like those who've experienced a trauma of some form. This separation was a trauma.

"Long Term Issues For the Adopted Child," Disorders and Issues: Adoption, American Addiction Centers, accessed on June 18, 2015, https://www.mentalhelp.net/articles/long-term-issues-for-the-adopted-child/.

"The Mental Health of U.S. Adolescents Adopted in Infancy," HHS Author Manuscripts, National Center for Biotechnology Information, U.S. National Library of Medicine, last updated June 20, 2015, https://www.ncbi.nlm.nih.gov/pmc/articles/PMC4475346/.

Chapter 8. Poor Folks

p. 54

4-H is America's largest youth development organization—empowering nearly six million young people across the U.S. with the skills to lead for a lifetime.

"About Nebraska 4-H," Institute of Agriculture and Natural Resources, accessed on December 26, 2003, https://4h.unl.edu/about.

Quotes in the Book

"More often the stopping point is the starting point."
— Tom Herzog, End Stigma Advocate

"The grace of God is a wind which is always blowing."
— Ramakrishna

"We meet and come together with those we love to work through our rough edges."
— Matt Kelley, Author

"It's a bit informal."
Mary Berry, a British food writer

"We must accept finite disappointment, but never lose infinite hope."
— Martin Luther King, Jr.

"Fate, destiny, and luck. Three words to some, three saviors to me. Any adopted child can tell you these words shape the core of our appreciation and embody our sense of vulnerability in the world. I was adopted at birth and I am a living story of fate, destiny and luck."
— Dillon Henry, The Dillon Henry Foundation

"Self-hatred and hopelessness stay with you like a shadow."
— Unknown

"Knowing your own darkness is the best method for dealing with the darknesses of other people."

— Carl Jung

"If you're honest with me then you're likely to be honest with 'we.'"

— Unknown A.A.

"This is a program of action; it's the doing not the wanting or needing."

— Unknown

"Change how you think, then your actions   will change."

— Bill R.

"You were sick, but now you're well again, and there's work to do."

— Kurt Vonnegut, Timequake

"Courage is not the absence of fear, but the capacity to act despite our fears."

— John McCain, U.S. Senator

"When I say to you from the bottom of my heart: YOU MATTER, I say this not to inspire you or make you feel better about yourself."

— Angela Maiers, Author, Educator & Speaker

"We will love you until you love yourself enough to care."

— A.A. Cathy

About the Author

Bryan Wempen is an author, speaker, and researcher. He is a certi-fied Mental Health First Aid Instructor working on several programs for training and speaking nationwide to corporations, first respond-ers, and veterans. He is also the author Note to Self: A Collection of 99 Life Lessons (2015) and Dancing with Big Data, Conversations with the Experts (2015). His 25 years in leadership, recruiting, and technology combined with 27 years of substance use provided him many exciting and colorful experiences. Bryan lives Kansas City with his wife, Michella, watching soccer, cycling, traveling, and drinking coffee.

Also by Bryan Wempen

'Note to Self' lessons are simple, useful living life suggestions. Bryan Wempen shares about living with an open mind and heart, working on his next chapter in sober life. His daily mantra: Rough days happen, they too shall pass.

On Sale Now

57360759R00090

Made in the USA
Columbia, SC
08 May 2019